Make Miracles Happen

Gayle

Now visionize the resolution to your visions... You have the power - Gayle now just do it.

Make Miracles Happen

✦

**Be Healthy, Prosperous, and Triumphant
Using Three Easy, Miracle-Provoking Exercises
Starting Now!**

Peter Copani

iUniverse, Inc.
New York Lincoln Shanghai

Make Miracles Happen
Be Healthy, Prosperous, and Triumphant Using Three Easy, Miracle-Provoking Exercises Starting Now!

iUniverse books may be ordered through booksellers or by contacting:

iUniverse
2021 Pine Lake Road, Suite 100
Lincoln, NE 68512
www.iuniverse.com
1-800-Authors (1-800-288-4677)

The Visionization® and Visionizing® brand and Make Miracles Happen™ are trademarks.

Layout and photo design by Michael N. Largent. Cover art and additional photos and illustrations by John P. D'Esposito. Editing by Kim Diaz, M.Ed./SAS Educational Consultant. Back cover photo of Mr. Copani by Faye Pessel Vassilatos. Space photos courtesy of NASA.

ISBN-13: 978-0-595-37970-5 (pbk)
ISBN-13: 978-0-595-82339-0 (ebk)
ISBN-10: 0-595-37970-2 (pbk)
ISBN-10: 0-595-82339-4 (ebk)

Printed in the United States of America

Conscious Co-creation, Self-Healing, Financial Independence,
and Problem-Solving

www.mindhealingmiracles.com

Make Miracles Happen is dedicated to my Spirit-Author,

to my son

Vincent Peter "John-Vince" Copani,

and to my two surrogate sons

John P. "John-Johnny" D'Esposito

and

Michael Nathan "Nate" Largent.

They have been a source of personal growth

and an inspiration.

"Everything that irritates us about others can lead us to an understanding of ourselves."

—*Carl Jung*

"I am a universal being, complete and healed and embodied as one mind/spirit self containing and reflecting the whole."

—*Peter Copani*

Contents

Preface

I started writing *Make Miracles Happen* decades ago as a tribute to the legacy of my son, John-Vince. Like me, he was a confused and troubled teenager. Generally uninterested in taking advice, he stubbornly wanted to learn everything for himself through his own personal experiences. Thus I learned to offer my lessons from life, my accumulated knowledge, and what I believe to be practical, fatherly advice solely as a way to assist others in exercising their own best judgment.

When I was thirteen and in despair—even on the brink of suicide—I prayed, "If I must live this life, then please let me be of use to others." Serving others became my purpose for living, not to mention a way to make a better life for my family, friends, neighbors, and maybe—just maybe—in some small way to contribute to making this a better world. My greatest hope is that *Make Miracles Happen* will be in some way useful to everyone who happens upon it.

Make Miracles Happen contains an effective, universal Visionizing® thought process that will empower *anyone who uses it*, especially those in a time of personal crisis or who are in need of a miracle. Read *Make Miracles Happen* if you would like to know who you are, where you came from, what you're doing here, and where you're going. You'll learn how to heal yourself, how to become financially independent, and how to be truly helpful to others. If you are experiencing a difficult period in your life and would like to make a change, are desperate and in need of financial or spiritual progress, have a serious personal relationship problem to resolve, or have a life-threatening disease and need a miracle, you will be guided toward your desired resolution—every step of the way!

This book presents important ancient wisdom along with modern scientific conclusions about a universal Visionizing thought process. After researching and studying what various "truth-seekers" throughout history had to say, I formulated a process of personal change using three tangible, easy-to-learn "miracle-provoking exercises" and "mind-healing steps." I analyzed my own true-life experiences and then proved the miracle-provoking exercises and steps to be effective for my friends and clients. The proof that the three miracle-provoking exercises, of which Visionizing is one, will work for you lies in you putting them to the test for yourself.

Through extensive experience, I discovered why Visionizing works for some people and not for others—an important point of contention in the verification of its potential.

In *Make Miracles Happen* I share how I beat cancer. I show my own personal change from a drug addict into "America's leading playwright of the streets" fame. I share how I went from being on welfare for the third time to becoming financially independent. This time-tested Visionizing thought process allowed me to heal a chronic back problem, overcome post-traumatic stress disorder, cure myself of hepatitis C, and remain pain-free despite arthritis at the back of my neck. Most important of all, I finally conquered the fear of death and gained peace of mind.

For thousands of years, this miracle-provoking Visionizing process has been proven effective by millions of people all over the world. Why not me? Why not you?

As you read this book, you will challenge every dogma, philosophy, and "law of the universe" in your belief system. You will venture into the unknown, expect the impossible, and seek to overcome all odds with inspired determination. Your success will come to feel tangible as you gain all you need to know and do to materialize your own personal miracles. In this book, I describe the miracle-provoking exercises as I do in the "Make Miracles Happen" live presentations and seminars.

The thought process used in *Make Miracles Happen* works in conjunction with universal and cosmic laws and involves a direct experience between each individual and God. Divine providence is the final arbiter. Only each individual himself or herself can be a witness to his or her own personal awakening (I take *awakening* and *healing* to be one and the same.) The practice or proof of this Visionizing thought process rests with each individual, who must prove or disprove the power of co-creative manifestation for himself or herself.

No guarantee whatsoever is made to anyone by me that this system of self-healing and manifestation, including but not limited to all *miracle-provoking* exercises and recommendations embodied in the process, will yield specific results or desired outcomes for any specific individual at anytime.

Make Miracles Happen is based on my research, mentoring, and practical experience. The information contained herein is in no way to be considered as a substitute for consultation with a duly licensed physician.

No single book, study, course, or seminar gave me the following three miracle-provoking exercises in the form in which I put them forth for you here. They have evolved solely as a result of my research, writing, mentoring, and putting them into practice. To more fully benefit, you are encouraged to project your own *desired resolution* of any personal health or prosperity challenge in the miracle-provoking exercises where applicable. If you are fortunate enough to have no such challenges right now, these exercises will help you maintain optimum health, increase your personal growth, serve others, gain peace of mind, or share more fully in the abundance of the universe.

It cost me thousands of dollars and decades of study time to come to the understandings, intricacies, and nuances of the processes described in this book. It is an honor and a privilege to have this opportunity to share them with you.

"Only a life lived for others is a life worthwhile."

—*Albert Einstein*

1

Truth-Seekers

One of my earliest childhood awarenesses was the distinct feeling that I had come from somewhere else. I felt separated from my "source" and had a longing to return. Feeling abandoned, I cried, "How do I get through living? I'm going to have to get through this life." Then came another realization: "I'm going to have to go through dying." It was as if I knew what death meant—as if I had been through it before. Distraught, I cried out in anguish: "Why am I here? I don't want to be here!"

When I could stop crying, I began to listen, objectively observing myself as if from outside my body. I saw a boy somewhere between three and six years old who was frightened, alone, and crouched under a kitchen sink in a dilapidated apartment.

Later, when I was transitioning from my teens to my twenties, I had a memorable dream in which I woke up in a gigantic cavern deep in the earth. It was filled with pathways. I was trying to decide which road or path among many that I should take. I saw long, short, high, low, twisted, straight, and winding paths—yet all of them led to an enormous aquarium protruding from the top of the cave. In it I could see bodies floating in what appeared to be formaldehyde. I was puzzled by the realization that no matter which path I chose, my body would end up in *there*! I was relieved to discover that it was only a fear of death dream. Or *was* it a dream?

In the 1960s, as a naïve "child of the universe" living in Greenwich Village, New York City, I had another memorable vision. At a dentist's office, I was given laughing gas before having a tooth extracted. I became fearful even as my body was strapped into the dentist's chair. I felt the wind at my ears, as if my bodiless spirit-self was moving through space. Suddenly, I felt peaceful as I moved toward a brilliant light in the distance. I enjoyed a peaceful anticipation, as if I were simply going home. Then I was stopped abruptly by two entities. One said, "You have to go back." I resisted defiantly. In a kind and understanding voice, the other said, "You can't go that way. You need to study this first." Suddenly, before me appeared a huge, thick book with the words *The World* printed on it. As I opened the book, it transformed into the spinning Earth. I was seeing the world from an outer-space perspective. Much to my amazement, I awoke in the dentist's recovery room—minus one tooth, but having gained an awesome near-death experience.

Knowing I had no way off the planet until I learned what was to be learned from *The World*, I trusted my intuitive self for survival from then on. I experimented with my emotions with the objective perspective of a research scientist and the inquisitiveness of a truth-seeker.

I had been raised dependent upon the earth, the son of sharecroppers on a farm in upstate New York. I had no idea of what the rest of the world was about. I felt earthbound and wanted to be "free." But how could I know what I wanted to do until I did it?

What I enjoyed most was the secure position of being an Objective Observer. I loved to just drift and observe people doing whatever they were doing. I felt detached, as though I were "out there" observing myself and the world instead of actually participating in it. I recognized the role of the Objective Observer as being my true self. It was like watching life on television. I loved to wander the streets of New York City. I witnessed acts of kindness contrasted with acts of cruelty in a mat-ter of minutes. What meaning could be found in all of this? I was in awe of human-ity and all of life, yet I was also painfully frightened of being involved in what at times appeared to be a cruel and threatening world.

I finally decided to become an actor. Acting allowed me to play various roles and to experience being many different people during one lifetime—although, I now understand, I was pretending to experience life without committing to any true involvement. Being an actor was enjoyable, but it didn't provide me with much of an income.

Eventually I was on welfare, feeling limited and vulnerable, and now longing to permanently leave the planet. At that time, a "rags-to-riches" friend named Tony gave me his secret to success: a book titled *The Lazy Man's Way to Riches* by Joe Karbo.

The book described a thought process—one that I found repeated, in some form or other, in every significant book I came to read. I later discovered it to be a simpli-fied and incomplete form of Visionizing. I became interested in the Visionizing process because it gave my objective thinking focus and because my friend Tony, who had also been a struggling actor, had totally changed his lifestyle and gone from poverty to riches.

I was less interested in making money than in searching for truth. More than anything, I desired to know the meaning of life: Who am I? Where did I come from? Why am I here? Where am I going?

Research

In my quest to know, I began to read and study. I explored Jewish scriptures; several versions of the New Testament; and particularly the book of Ruth and the Essene Bible. I delved into the lives and works of Moses, Jesus, Buddha, Gandhi, Mohammed, and Krishna. My favorite movies were *Ben Hur* and *The Ten Commandments.*

I chanted "Nam Myoho Renge Kyo, Nam Myoho Renge Kyo," words from the Lotus Sutra, 500 B.C., India. Nam Myoho Renge Kyo is chanted for enlightenment. It has been translated to mean, "I believe in cause and effect and in the oneness of the universe."

My studies of ancient truth and its seekers included the Kabbalah, astrology, and the teachings of Socrates, Plato, Aristotle, and Pythagoras, who translated numbers into form to "know thyself." I read all of Kahlil Gibran—author of *The Prophet,* who tells us, "Your life is your religion"—and all of Emanuel Swedenborg, who said almost 300 years ago that although human beings appear to be separate from one another, we're all connected in a cosmic unity.

Swedenborg's writing served as a spiritual guide for Helen Keller, among many others. Deaf, blind, and originally mute—although, incredibly, she did learn to speak—Helen Keller was my inspiration. If Helen Keller could overcome her earthly challenges, why couldn't I?

In Search of a Miracle

In 1972, three doctors diagnosed me with testicular cancer.

I wound up in the poverty ward of St. Vincent's Hospital in Manhattan. The surgeon described for me the three-to seven-hour operation: "We're going to cut across, two inches above your pubic area, Peter, and down the sides. We make a flap…go in that way….Please sign this release giving us permission to have student observers…"

"No one mentioned student observers before!" I blurted out. "I'm very shy!"

The surgeon continued. "…and to remove any suspicious tumors or organs."

"Remove organs?" I said. I was horrified. "I'm not prepared for a sex change!" Trying to remain calm, I asked, "Doctor, please. What are my alternatives?"

"Umm…cancer and death."

It seemed I had no practical choice but to sign it, so I did.

As the doctor left, I noticed two derelicts drinking whiskey from a bottle. One started in gleefully playing with the controls on the next bed, saying, "Up, down, heh-heh…down, up." The patient in the bed, who looked like he was recovering from surgery, was in a panic, his eyes bulging and his head rolling from side to side. "Uhhh!" he moaned. "Ahhh. Ahhh!"

A nurse stood right there between the beds, calmly staring at a blank wall.

I heard my objective intuitive internal voice say, "Peter, get out of there." I was thinking that I would be the victim of those derelicts by the next morning. I envisioned myself speaking in what I imagined to be the high-pitched voice of a eunuch.

In a panic, I jumped out of bed, fumbling to get that stupid robe off. The nurse approached. "You can't just leave," she said. "What about your testicles?"

"I'm taking them with me!"

The nurse called out, "This patient needs to be sedated!"

I grabbed my jeans and ran for it—like the human guinea pig in *The Planet of the Apes*. The chase was on. I dashed down the stairs and barged out an emergency exit. I was blinded by the bright sunshiny day. An alarm sounded "Whoop, Whoop!" as the door shut behind me. Visions of being sedated and brought back in a straitjacket for the surgery filled my mind.

There I was—this very shy guy—running as fast as possible down Seventh Avenue in Greenwich Village still clutching my jeans.

And what do people do when they see a naked guy running toward them? They drop their mouths open and stare!

I finally ducked into an entranceway, shuffled into my jeans, and, pretending to be someone else, hastily continued home.

I was relieved to be out of that hospital, but did I do the best thing? I felt embarrassed, humiliated, terrified, and in need of a miracle! Trembling, almost unaware of what I was doing, I began Visionizing in prayer—that is, seeing myself healed, with all my parts whole and attached. "Oh please, dear God, please!"

Within our minds we have a creative device capable of bringing pain, misery, and poverty; of this I'm positive. The same creative force is also capable of bringing healing, prosperity, and miracles through the process of Visionizing. *This* I had to prove. I wanted never to wind up in a poverty ward again!

Exploring Deeper

I searched through and researched the products of the minds of hundreds of history's truth-seekers. I explored medicine, science, and philosophy and writings about self-help, positive thinking, and psychology, including the works of Sigmund Freud, Carl Jung, Hermann Hesse and Wilhelm Reich. Edgar Cayce—referred to as "the Sleeping Prophet"—and his work helped me to understand practical metaphysics.

Other books from which I benefited included:

- Norman Vincent Peale's *The Power of Positive Thinking*

- Karl Menninger's *The Human Mind*

- L. Ron Hubbard's many works on Scientology

- Dale Carnegie's *How to Win Friends and Influence People*

- Bernie Siegel's *Love, Medicine and Miracles*

- Elisabeth Kübler-Ross's *On Death and Dying*

- Neale Donald Walsch's *Conversations with God*

- Gary Zukav's *The Seat of the Soul*

I also explored medical scientist Bruce Lipton's research on integrating quantum physics with cell biology. In-depth studies were warranted for *The Holographic Universe* by Michael Talbot and *The Looking Glass Universe* by John C. Briggs and F. David Peat. Finally, I marveled at *A Course in Miracles* by Helen Schucman, a Columbia University professor who wrote of taking dictation from a spirit-author identifying himself as Jesus.

I had expanded my thinking from the story of creation through the theory of evolution, from Einstein's relativity through quantum physics and on to a holographic paradigm. Finally, I put the ancient wisdom and modern scientific discoveries, along with my own personal experience, into the perspective of *A Course in Miracles*.

Gaining bits and pieces from the various authors who presented their own versions of this thought process, I had discovered through this research the Visionization process. I was never quite sure if I was doing it right or whether I would get my desired resolution. Later I learned through trial and error how the miracle-provoking exercises and mind-healing steps that were evolving in my mind could come into focus and be applied in anyone's life.

"Employ your time in improving yourself by other men's writings, so that you shall gain easily what others have labored hard for."

—Socrates

2

The First Miracle-Provoking Exercise

Our *first miracle-provoking exercise* is helpful in stimulating creativity and gaining a collective perspective of our mind in relation to our physical self, the universe, and the Creative Energy Force or nondenominational God.

Stimulating Creativity

Begin by taking a deep breath. Focus on the images that surface in your mind as you imagine the following.

Imagine the perimeter of your body expanding into the totality of the entire universe.

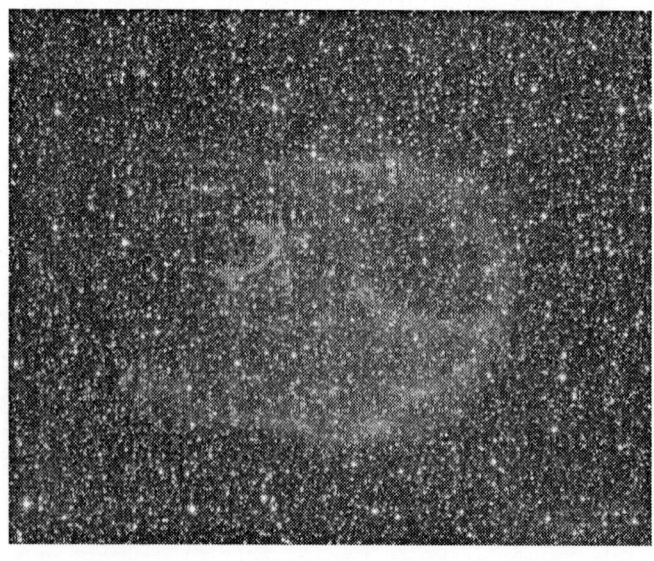

When creating a vision the verbiage must always be in the first person. Think, "My powerful and magnificent body cells are expanding into the powerful and magnificent stars of the universe! My glands, muscles, organs, bones, and systems are transforming into galaxies and solar systems."

Scientists tell us that the universe pulsates. Imagine the entire body of the universe pulsating to the beat of your heart. The black holes are the pores in your skin. The happenings of the entire universe are taking place inside your mind/body/universe.

We are and remain the Objective Observer. Please think along with me now: "My trillions of body cells have become stars. My liver—the Milky Way! I am free of all fear.

Say it as though you could believe it: "I am free of all fear!"

In your Objective Observer eye, see, feel, and be this awesome and most powerful mind/body/universe. You consist of energy, atoms, space, gases, trillions of star cells, galaxies, asteroids, comets, planets, and moons—all functioning in harmony as one.

Gaining a Collective Perspective

Please think along with me now: "I am a universal being, complete and healed and united as one 'mind/body/spirit-cell' in the body of the universe, sharing in the collective consciousness of a magnificent Creative Energy Force."

Push any fears aside. Breathe deeply. Take a moment here to see, feel, and just be your naked (bodiless) spirit self. Take a moment to think, "I am an awesome universal being."

Oneness

Now imagine the total *outer-world* Creative Energy Force universe imploding back into your mind's body as rapidly as the perimeter of your mind's body expanded into it.

Our Objective Observer, our naked spirit-self remains a fragment of the universal Creative Energy Force. Like a fragment of a hologram, this Objective Observer-self, or fragment of the Creative Energy Force in each of us, appears to be separate; yet, it contains and reflects the whole or entire universe. This brings us to the immediate recognition that our Objective Observer naked spirit-self is not separate from our Source, Creator, God, or any name you prefer to call this power. We are one part of the whole.

Establishing who you are in relation to your Creator is the most important factor in co-creation. By uniting with the Creative Energy Force that ignites your vision, you are manifesting or projecting it into what appears to be the outer world.

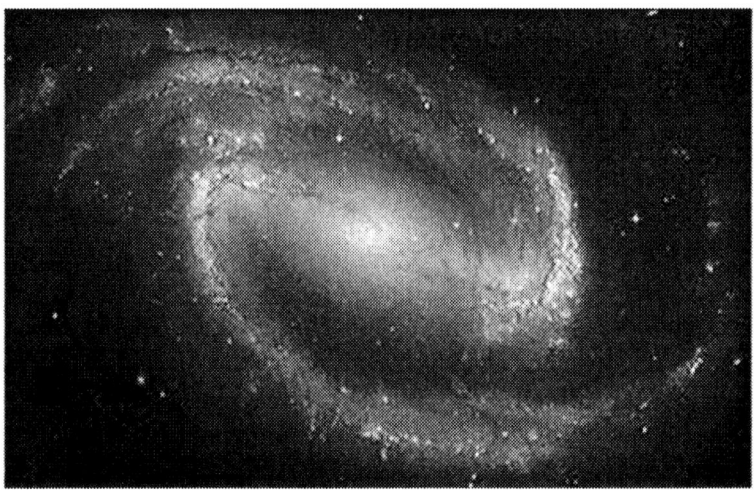

"You have set yourselves a difficult task, but you will succeed if you persevere; and you will find a joy in overcoming obstacles—a delight in climbing rugged paths, which you would perhaps never know if you did not sometime slip backward—if the road was always smooth and pleasant. Remember, no effort that we make to attain something beautiful is ever lost. Sometime, somewhere, somehow we shall find that which we seek."

—Helen Keller

3

How Miracles Happen: The Second Miracle-Provoking Exercise

The Inner World is all that pertains to our Objective Observer naked spirit-self, like silence and observation. The Outer World is all that is separate, detached, or beyond our naked spirit-self such as illusions. Ideas, thoughts, perceptions, and visions, which can originate from either the ego mind thought system or the universal mind thought system, are subject to the Creative Force mechanism of our minds. Like communication centers, our minds connect our Outer and Inner worlds.

The Inner World and Outer World are related: we can't change the world from out there in the Outer World, but we can change our Outer World through Visionizing which takes place in our Inner World. Our Inner World consists of our visions projected, whereas the Outer World contains our physical bodies, or objects such as our cars or houses, is thought of as external and separate.

A miracle is a change in perception. To begin the second miracle-provoking exercise, we will need to attempt a dramatic change in our perceptions.

Radically changing perceptions can put our problems, challenges, or triumphs into perspective. Better understanding the Inner World/Outer World relationship is the goal of the following experience.

Put your hands up to the sides of your head about five inches away from your ears with palms facing toward the back of your head and say, to yourself or aloud, "Inner World." Then, while stretching your arms out in front of you, turn your hands so your palms are facing away from my face, and think or say, "Project." Next, turn your palms toward each other at a slant as if making a presentation of whatever is before you. While your arms are still extended, say, "Outer World" while bringing your hands together touching pinkies, then separating them as if what is before you is on display; think or say, "Observe."

By engaging in these physical gestures, you are observing an incident that has appeared to have happened in the outer world and asking:

- "What is the lesson or purpose in this?"

- "What is it in me causing this?"

- "What am I to learn from this?"

Repeat this action several times. Practice searching your mind for an awareness of a lesson or purpose inherent in any personal challenge or upsetting situation in your life. You may wish to take a moment now to do this.

The "Inner World: Project. Outer World: Observe" (IWP-OWO) exercise is both simple and powerful. Do it a few times until the acronym IWP-OWO allows you to immediately imagine or perform the movement along with the words. Repeat this exercise until the answer surfaces. You will, sooner or later, gain a new perspective on any action, situation, event, or challenge. Later in the book, you will have several opportunities to use this IWP-OWO second miracle-provoking exercise.

Many truth-seekers tell us that the Outer World is a cause, and we are the effect. This way of thinking accepts the ego mind thought system. It emphasizes the separateness of everything, from individual people to all Creation. You have a problem? It's because of what your parents or the planets did or didn't do. Or your problem stems from your genes and DNA. Or it's because of what the government did or didn't do…or any number of other reasons. In this ego mind thought system, which emphasizes separateness, you are special and separate. You're *not* responsible for what happens to you. You are a victim of circumstance.

However, other truth-seekers tell us just the opposite. Many spiritual seekers have written that our Inner World is the cause and the Outer World is the effect. That's what the IWP-OWO exercise reveals. What you are observing out there is a reflection or manifestation of what is taking place in the Inner World of your mind. Such an explanation emphasizes the universal mind thought system of oneness. We are one with each other and all Creation. Therefore, it's *what we did or didn't do* that is the root cause of all our problems.

We are neither defined simply by the ego mind or the universal mind. We have access to them, but we are not "them." They are not "ours." They are thought systems unto themselves. We merely choose to subscribe to one or the other system at any given time.

I very often recognize the ego mind dancing in protest in my family, friends, clients, and in myself. It says: "I didn't cause all this pain and suffering from my backache, my arthritis, my heart disease, my high cholesterol, my low cholesterol, my hepatitis C (HCV). I didn't cause my own cancer! I didn't do that to myself...did I?"

The Visionizing® Process

One day when I was about twelve years old, I decided to define myself as "special and separate," by skipping school. To avoid attending, I came up with false evidence in an effort to make a pretended illness appear real. "I got a headache," I said. "Oh, it hurts...ow!" I really got into it.

When I was ready to see, feel, and be this poor innocent victim, I telephoned the office. "Hello, this is Peter Copani. I won't be in school today. I got a headache. Oh, I think it's a migraine!...Ow!"

"If you feel better, you can come in this afternoon. Or, we'll see you tomorrow morning, Peter," said the secretary.

"Yeah…OK." I hung up feeling proud of my deception. But then all this play turned into something much more sinister.

While rehearsing, repeating, and feigning the illness, acting as if it were taking place in the present power-moment of now, I had unknowingly Visionized it. It imprinted. By mid-afternoon that day, I was feeling guilty for having perpetrated a fraud, and I had a pounding headache. Did I do it to myself?

Once a vision imprints in the Creative Force, it's going to manifest.

Imprint. An impression, mark, or fix made firmly and permanently in the Creative Force to influence a result or action. You make an imprint in the Creative Force by passionately repeating affirmatives.

Affirmative. A message, statement, or directive made firmly to yourself. It must be personal and in the first person. It is your self-talk, be it silent or spoken.

What is Visionizing?

Visionizing® is a process that combines the positive thinking popularized in the 1950s, the euphoric daydreaming of the 1960s, the goal-setting of the 1970s, the affirmations or self-talk promoted in the 1980s, and imaging or visualizing of the 1990s. It is not any one of them alone, but rather a cocktail or combination of all of them, plus the utilization of the natural learning process of repetition condensed in the present power-moment of now.

Visionizing® begins with a vision: a vividly clear mental motion-picture, starring you. Your vision must involve a personal incident, real or imagined, intensified with emotions and sensations, as if it were taking place in the present power-moment of now. Visionizing means repeating this process until it imprints and manifests or comes into being!

Going further, you may wish to practice Visionizing in prayer. Visionizing in prayer means to pray or speak with your Creator in the way you ordinarily do according to your own personal or religious persuasion, but all the while you are seeing, feeling, and being the resolution to your request during the present power-moment of your praying.

Now is the "power-moment"—because now is the only time you actually have. The past is full of "nows" gone by. As Earl Nightingale put it, "now, and it's gone; now, and it's gone." Only in the present "now" do you have the power to act. The future depends on your actions or inactions in the present power-moment of now.

Five Types of Visions

There are five types of visions: inspiration, revelation, neglect, desperation, and perseverance.

- **Visions born of inspiration** are natural and spontaneous. When your vision is inspired, the imprint is strong and dominant. No conscious repetition is required.

- **Visions born of revelation** are when a striking disclosure is made and/or provoked through probing and determination. This kind of vision is very often the kind that results from using the IWP-OWO miracle-provoking exercise.

- **Visions born of neglect** take place when a person is vulnerable, unaware, or lazy and allows just any information—true or untrue, beneficial or harmful—to imprint in the Creative Force without the person's knowledge or selective effort.

- **Visions born of desperation** come out of the pain and desperation of the moment. This type of vision is also immediate, because the desperation acts as a catalyst to make a dominant imprint that you are driven to repeat.

- **Visions born of perseverance** are the kind of Visionizing described in detail below and in Chapter IV, which explains the third miracle-provoking exercise. This final category of visions is the only kind we can deliberately or consciously co-create.

Visions Born of Perseverance

Creating visions born of perseverance requires that you take several steps. Decide what you would like your vision to be. In my example of skipping middle school, my decision was to envision a headache.

1. Develop the appropriate affirmatives. In my example, the affirmative "I have a headache" was appropriate for skipping school.

2. Repeat the affirmatives for action until they imprint. This could mean repeating them thousands of times. You may find that your vision is being resisted or is not manifesting in a reasonable amount of time—anywhere

from immediately to a few decades, depending upon the scope of the vision you are creating.

3. Be aware of and abandon any opposing information that surfaces. In my skipping school example, I put aside any thoughts of being healthy.

4. Dominate the opposing information with positive repeated affirmatives for action. The affirmative "I have a headache" helped bring about the desired result of getting out of having to go to school.

5. Listen to your subconscious inner voice to recognize new opportunities until your result is present. As a schoolboy, I repeated my performance in my mind until "I have a headache" imprinted in the subconscious Creative Force. Imprinting made it dominant, causing the affirmative to overpower any "I am healthy" thoughts—and clearing the way for a genuine painful headache to manifest.

We will go through the creation of visions born of perseverance in the following exercises so you have the opportunity to experience for yourself how to use this part of the Visionizing® process.

The Creative Force

Now we're going to focus in on the Creative Force—the key to how and why the Visionizing® process works. The Creative Force is a learning device used by our Objective Observer spirit-self. Like a movie projector, the Creative Force is a neutral device. It doesn't distinguish between the ego mind or the universal mind, Outer World or Inner World, fantasy or reality, or our fears or desires; furthermore, it doesn't recognize when we're pretending or joking.

Once any vision is imprinted in the Creative Force, it becomes a belief whether it happens to be true or false!

The Function of the Creative Force

The function of the Creative Force is to take our visions and project them. The imprinting arises from the union of the vision with the "light" in the movie projector–like Creative Force. Your imprinted vision and the light of the Creative Force combine to co-create and display a manifestation. The light is representative of the Creative Energy Force, a term for the nondenominational God—the source of all creation.

An imprinted vision most often manifests or comes into being long after you have forgotten the cause of that initial imprinting.

So, what does this mean?

It means that today's illnesses, challenges, problems, and triumphs are a result of our thinking that took place maybe five, ten, fifteen, or twenty years ago. Their origins could be back in our childhood or infancy. Some truth-seekers tell us they go back to past lives!

The ego mind thought system is part of this equation. Aspiring to be our god, the ego mind thought system is most identifiable in the cunning and cruelty inherent in sibling rivalry: the competition for the love of mother, father, God, and country. We can also view this ego mind as being cloaked in the legal and religious robes of respectability. The height of ego minded arrogance is reached by those who create unjust laws and false gods—in their own ego mind image and then have the audacity to use their deities and codes of behavior—to control others.

This self-aggrandizing ego mind or shadow self, as Carl Jung called it, uses all forms of fear, seduction, and trickery to hold us in its false system of thought, where separation from our creator and from each other manifests guilt. Guilt demands punishment; punishment manifests fear; and fear of punishment manifests masochism, insanity, and suicide.

So how are we going to get rid of all this ego mind guilt so it doesn't drive us nuts?

Our ego tells us to "project it out—find a scapegoat!" So we look to our brothers and sisters. In this way, hate, prejudice, and sadism are manifested. Then, if we follow through, we attack, punish, or kill the scapegoat to justify our actions. Thus, we imagine we can remain an "innocent" and avoid any punishment forthcoming.

The ego mind doesn't tell us that when we project the guilt, it *boomerangs*.

The IWP-OWO Learning Process in Action

The images, feelings, and visions of our Inner World are projected into the Outer World, what many truth-seekers refer to as the dream world of illusions. An Inner world Outer World learning process requires observation and experience. Please recall the IWP-OWO second miracle-provoking exercise: Inner World—project; Outer World—observe.

But wait...uh-oh. Think about your inner visions. What are we projecting? It's our guilt coming back. From the Inner World feeling envy, greed, and revenge, which we project into the Outer World. There we observe murder, terror, and war! Our Inner World feels specialness; our projected Outer World reflects illness. "Oh, stop!" we say. Our Inner World observes time, our Outer World mirrors aging. "Oh, no!" Our Inner World preserves separateness, our Outer world admits death. "Get me out of here! Help! I'm trapped inside a human body!"

We're in this dream world of illusions because of a subconscious decision to be separate from oneness with the Creative Energy Force and oneness of each other.

Birth, by causing us to be defined by the perimeter of our bodies, is a manifestation of this psychological split into the ego mind, consisting of specialness and separateness.

Truth-seekers as far back as the ancient Egyptians and as recent as scientists at the cutting edge agree: we are not this ego mind body! It's an illusion—the figure in the dream, as Freud would say.

Other truth-seekers tell us that the entire outer world is an illusion. The Outer World is created by our Objective Observer's powerful Creative Force within us—but created *collectively*, meaning by a collective consciousness. Our purpose in this book is to learn a lesson, activate a change, and encourage our progress or growth. Visionizing is a device for us to discover "who we are, where we came from, why we're here, and where we're going."

Many truth-seekers say that God created everything—the good, the bad, and the ugly. Some believe that the collective Objective Observer spirit-self is the One Son of God. In other words, we are all as cells in the body of creation that is "the One Son of God." Others tell us that God created the One Son and we, being the One Son, created the rest of this universe; that is why it is referred to as an illusion. Most truth-seekers agree we are the unlimited Spirit, the Objective Observer, an immortal fragment of a universal hologram, with the freedom of choice between the limited ego mind experience and the unlimited universal mind thought system.

If you are in your ego mind body, as most of us are much of the time, guilt and fear will surface. These are merely "manipulative me" ego "attack" thoughts that pop into our mind: thoughts of unworthiness, arrogance, lack, jealousy, anger, revenge, envy, lust, greed, illness, and death.

Our decision-making Objective Observer fragment of a universal hologram has the power to clear these attack thoughts and replace them with universal mind thoughts:

• oneness with each other and all creation;

- wholeness, meaning freedom from guilt;

- abundance, meaning freedom from want or need;

- and immortality, meaning freedom from fear—even fear of death.

Freedom of Choice

Our Objective Observer naked spirit-self, fragment of the Creative Energy Force, can choose—and it is a choice—to be in the universal mind thought system of oneness or in the ego mind thought system of separateness. We can't be in both oneness and separateness at the same time. Like lightness and darkness, one cancels the other out.

It is this choosing that will determine whether the visions imprinted in our Creative Force will be those that manifest pain, misery, and poverty, or those that manifest healing, prosperity, and miracles.

In this chapter, we have seen that on some level or other we are responsible for everything that happens to us in our lives. We are also given choices, a mechanism by which those choices operate, and the power to manifest whatever we choose into our reality. "We are the children of God, co-creators of our world." We have the freedom of choice, be it consciously or unconsciously. The experiences of our lives are truly direct results of our choices. If you are not content with what you are experiencing—choose again!

"*Carefully watch your thoughts, for they become your words. Manage and watch your words, for they will become your actions. Consider and judge your actions, for they have become your habits. Acknowledge and watch your habits, for they shall become your values. Understand and embrace your values, for they become your destiny.*"

—*Mahatma Gandhi*

4

Visionizing: The Third Miracle-Provoking Exercise

Visionizing and conscious co-creation are one and the same. The only control you can take over your thought process is to deliberately program or construct your desired visions: those would be visions born of perseverance. Then, Vision-ize them until they imprint in the device of your Creative Force.

You have a choice as to what these visions will be. This freedom of choice is a determining factor in directing the course of your life.

Within your freedom to choose are both the obstacles you must overcome and the lessons you must learn to make your life smoother. Your future is firmly held in your present visions, whether you are consciously aware of them or not.

The third miracle-provoking exercise is Visionizing whatever makes you better off. In just a moment, we will Visionize the resolution to your health challenge. (Even if you don't have a health challenge, you can Visionize optimum health.) So let's put it to the test!

But first of all, I'm assuming that you in fact do *desire* to be healthy. Many people in the ego mind thought system find a benefit in being the sickly victim. As a result, being the victim gets imprinted in our subconscious Creative Force, most often unknowingly. In many cases, those inflicted with this imprint are unwilling or fearful to give it up! After all, less is expected of you, you get "special" treatment, and you can gain sympathy—considered a form of love to some people. By playing the victim, you can cause others to feel guilt. Their guilt motivates them to give you what you want. A child may play hurt or sick to get attention, or an adult may go see numerous doctors because he or she wants to reap the benefits from the money he or she paid for health insurance. I once heard a woman say, "I *better* get sick after I paid all that money for insurance." She laughed at her joke, but we know that the Creative Force does not distinguish between whether we are serious or joking. It imprints it all.

I often fly between New York City and Florida. I'm not the only one to notice those lines of ten to twenty people in wheelchairs who are pre-boarding—all lined up to be the first ones on the plane. Immediately after the plane lands, an announcement is made for those needing a wheelchair or special assistance to remain seated until everyone has deplaned. Something miraculous happens. Much to the amazement of flight attendants and other observant passengers, all but one or two of them stand up and rush to be among the first ones off the plane. This is emblematic of how we can make ourselves sicker or healthier to reap benefits or rewards. A dear friend, now eighty years young, admitted to me that he enjoyed the special attention. "Everyone is so nice to me, and it only cost me five bucks for what I call the wheelchair VIP service." After we laughed about it, he also admitted to feeling guilty. Sheepishly, he said, "It can be a long walk through the airport to the plane." At one time or another, we have all been guilty of such behaviors and rationalizations, which are characteristic of the ego mind thought system.

Recently, a client complained to me every time I saw her about the pain in her knee. Her doctor had said that she needed an operation. With a pathetic look on her face, she would beg me to visit her during her convalescence. I said I probably wouldn't be able to. Then, several months later, she told me that her doctor said he would not have to operate after all, and she added immediately, "Well, I did get that card so now I can park in handicapped spaces." She never mentioned the pain in her knee again. We can see this as another good example of how we sometimes make ourselves sicker or healthier to reap the benefits.

A friend in his mid-twenties told me that he'd have to retire early because he expected to have arthritis in his hands when he got older—"just like my mother." I answered, "I'm absolutely sure you will." Why? Because we move in the direction of our most dominant thoughts. Since these thoughts are the cause, it would naturally follow that the effect in this case would be arthritis in his hands.

Please keep two things in mind: A vision is a vividly clear mental motion picture, involving a personal incident, real or imagined, intensified with emotions and sensations, and taking place in the present power-moment of now. Second, major illnesses such as cancer and heart disease do not arise overnight. They develop over long periods of time. In many cases, it can take long periods of time to reverse the process and undo the disease.

Biologists have proven that just as we, cells in the body of creation, communicate with one another, our body cells communicate with each other as well. Imagine each of your trillions of body cells saying, "I'm healthy...I'm healthy...I'm healthy!" Now imagine these cells repeating such affirmatives right through the seven-year replication cycle, when every cell in every organ, gland, muscle, bone, and tendon in your entire body is replaced with new cells. Your cell replication process is in progress this very minute. Each of our approximately thirty trillion cells contains thousands of peptide receptors. Our visions affect the nature or temperament of our cells through these peptide cell receptors. In turn, our cells determine the temperament of our physical and mental well-being.

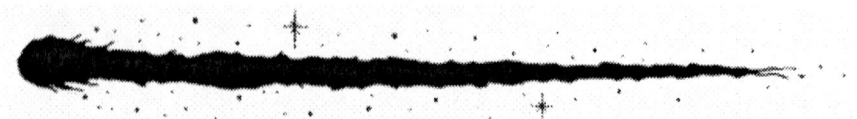

Visionizing the Resolution to Your Health Challenge

Now it's time to create a vision born of perseverance. Please say, either to yourself or aloud, "I'm healthy!" Say it as though you believe it at your deepest core: "I'm healthy." Say or think, "I'm pain-free!" and then, "I'm healthy and pain-free!"

Just repeating the words is *not* Visionizing! You need to focus on your desired result of being healthy, thinking or speaking in the first person, *while simultaneously* making a vividly clear mental picture of your entire "body self." Keep forefront in your vision any glands, organs, systems, or areas that are particularly afflicted. See them as healed, healthy, and whole. Forget about any ailments now.

In your mind's eye, see your lungs operative, pink, and clear of any congestion. Breathe!

Please think along with me again: "My healthy heart is pumping wholesome and nourishing blood through my perfectly functioning heart valves and plaque-free arteries, veins, and capillaries. My muscles are relaxed and free of pain. My skin is hydrated and supple. My bones are strong. I can hear and see clearly. I have an excellent long-and short-term memory. My immune system is alert and effective." See, feel, and be it.

Imagine eating and drinking organic or fresh, wholesome, and nourishing foods. What we eat is purported by many nutritionists to be the source or major cause of about ninety percent of all disease. These truth-seekers tell us that disease (remember: "dis-ease") is a direct result of what we put into our mouth and through our digestive and elimination systems. You may choose to supplement your Visionizing with a combination of fasting and exercising to gain or maintain optimum health. Whatever you choose to do will be more effective if you do it while Visionizing the desired resolution.

Now focus on your digestive system, beginning with your mouth, teeth, saliva, tongue, throat, stomach, and all supportive tissues, glands, and organs, like the liver and kidneys, right through to the intestines, colon, and out spouts, all functioning in harmony with each other.

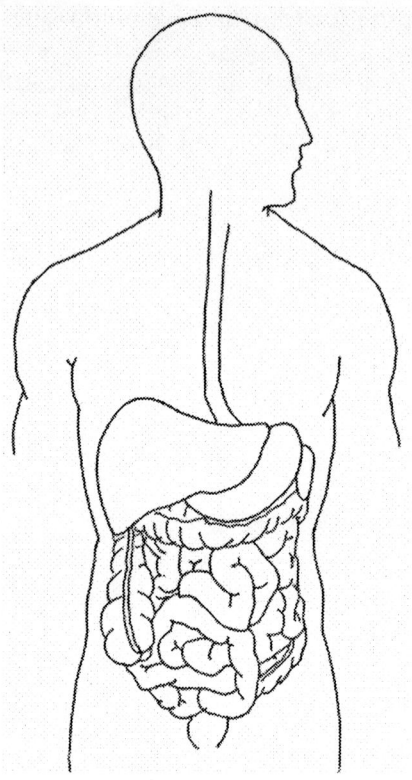

Forget about any ailments now. Focus on the desired resolution—being healthy—instead of any problem.

It's easy, once you decide to take control of your thoughts.

Now we need to add emotion to simultaneously imprint with our vividly clear picture. So, while doing the above, concentrate on *enjoying* being this vital and balanced healthy vision of you, the care-receiver, in the present power-moment of now. Your body's cells are "turned on" by the emotional component of the vision you are creating in your mind's eye.

What else do you feel while Visionizing yourself healed, healthy, and whole? When you are cured of any disease, wouldn't you most likely feel relief, gratitude, and appreciation? Sure! Add them to your mix.

Think in the first person again: "I am free of all pain and suffering." Imagine your brain releasing your body's own natural pain-killing endorphins to soothe any painful sensations. Breathe deeply and think: "I am free of all harmful sugar, nicotine, drugs, alcohol, and emotional addictions. I am free from all harmful yeast, fungus, mold, bacteria, and viral infections."

Think: "I am free of all attack thoughts, like anger and revenge. Every time I have an attack thought, I immediately overpower it by Visionizing positive healing and benevolent visions." A way to overpower through benevolence is to Visionize, "I am kind, considerate, loving, and lovable." You must envision *enjoying* the act of being kind, considerate, loving, and lovable. Just saying the words doesn't work.

In your mind's eye, hold the healthy image of yourself as you say, "Every cell in my body *is* healthy, now!"

At this point in one of my seminars, a woman stood and shouted, "I can't do this…I can't lie…because I know I'm sick!"

Well, listen to that affirmation. What we are doing while Visionizing is creating a projection—a living mental picture or future vision. Remember, *we move in the direction of our most dominant projections!* We are using Visionizing as medication to promote healing.

I told her, "Please be seated and just enjoy the vision of yourself being healthy now. Can you do that? Because I think that's the result you want, isn't it?" She thought for a moment. I went on: "Enjoy your thoughts now. We move in the direction of our fortified thoughts, which are these visions we're attempting to imprint in our Creative Force. Enjoy your visions of being healthy. It's greater than you think. Enjoy yourself. Enjoy yourself." I told her she could even sing and dance it: "Yes, as Maria did in *West Side Story*." Would you believe I actually sang and did a little dance step for her? "I feel healthy, oh so healthy! It's amazing how healthy I feel." She smiled. "That's healing. Even if your visions don't materialize immediately, you'll at least get the enjoyment out of this power-moment of doing it now!" She sat up and smiled broadly.

You can also practice the supportive soothing and healing acts of smiling, laughter, singing, swaying, rocking, or dancing.

Hold a picture of a healthy, triumphant, smiling you for the imprinting…"Smile. I'm going to take your picture." I made like I was holding and looking through the eye of a video camera. "That's it. Give me a nice big smile—good!" By starring in this vividly clear motion picture of health, you are in effect making a film, video, or DVD that will enable the Creative Force to illuminate your vision with light and project it. Remember, your imprinted vision and the light co-create; they reveal a…manifestation.

For the Caregiver

If you are a professional healthcare giver or have a loved one who is in need of a healing or miracle, you can follow this same process. Include a vision of your care-receiver healed, healthy, and whole. That's the only difference. Everything else is the same, in the first person. You still say, "I'm healthy!" Always interact with your healthcare recipient as though he or she is one with you in your vision of being healthy and whole. Your care-receiver is included when you see, feel, and are at one with them in your mind's eye, because you *are* one spirit-self. The healing power is in the unity of spiritual oneness. This will become clearer to you as we move forward.

How Visionizing Works

As we have seen, Visionizing calls upon the Creative Energy Force within to co-create your imprinted visions and manifest future happenings in your life. This process of Visionizing—from "realizing vision"—causes real, biological-based events. Repetition causes the neurons in your brain to form a network of neuron-tentacles that form a thought pattern, habit, or imprint. Think "djzz-djzz"—the sound of your electromagnetic brain impulses—"djzz-djzz"—lightning flashing in our imprinting of a vision brainstorm! "Djzz-djzz."

Along with repetition, the emotional component triggers our internal chemical factory, the hypothalamus gland, to secrete peptides that correspond to the emotion or sensation in our vision.

When our vision and corresponding emotions are simultaneously activated or imprinted by our Visionizing, our cell receptors *welcome* the corresponding peptide. This changes the temperament of the cell in favor of your vision. When the balance of compatible cells shifts in favor of your present vision, you are put on auto-control to do whatever is necessary to manifest your most dominant imprinted vision.

It is not the *words* that communicate the message to be imprinted in your creative force. It is the images and the emotions that the words invoke in your mind that become the bearers of your desired resolution to be manifested.

Hypochondriacs, beware! This same process is responsible for developing disease and harmful addictions. We're all addicts. We can become addicted to anything, including emotions. Some of us become addicted to anger or bitterness. And don't forget those sugar highs! Why not become addicted to being healthy, prosperous, and triumphant?

Remember, you have a choice as to what your visions born of perseverance will be. This freedom of choice is a determining factor in directing the course of your own life. It is *this choosing* that will determine whether the visions imprinted in your Creative Force will be those that manifest pain, misery, and poverty, or those that manifest healing, prosperity, and miracles. Use the third miracle-provoking exercise of the Visionizing process to create a triumphant and healthy you.

Personal Testimony: A Healing Miracle

In 1981, I couldn't walk because of an excruciatingly painful chronic back problem. All my life I had been familiar with back pain. My father, brother, and nephew all had operations on their lower backs. Bengay, chiropractors, and prescription painkillers would only temporarily relieve my symptoms but never resolve the problem. I finally accepted back pain as being part of my life. Was it because of my family's genes or DNA?

I decided to put Visionizing to the test.

I chose to be in the universal mind by calling upon the nondenominational God or Creative Energy Force. "Please show me how. When I am united in you, there is no obstacle to my peace." I Visionized®, "I am free of all pain."

You hear or read about miracles happening to other people all the time. Or maybe you watch "It's a Miracle" on television. "Well, why not me?" I thought.

I had been affirming every day for three years. What was I doing wrong? I was repeating the words "I'm healthy," every morning, noon, and night. But was I simultaneously repeating them with emotion and Visionizing® in the present power-moment of now? I don't think so!

Driven by determination, I took my cane and walked down my four flights of stairs—"oww...the pain!"—and then walked about twelve short blocks.

With each step, I Visionized, "My back is healed now! I'm pain-free!" I remembered to picture myself pain-free and healthy and to breathe deeply. "Every muscle, tendon, disk, and nerve is healthy and functioning in harmony. My back is healed now!" And yes, it's very difficult to Visionize when you're in pain!

With each step, I repeated, "I'm healthy now!" Then I would breathe deeply. See it, feel it, be it. I focused on my desired resolution of being pain-free, along with Visionizing my desired outcome. It became natural for me to feel relief and think, "Oh, God, thank you!"

As I climbed the stairs, I noticed that the sharp pain had diminished to a dull numbness. The numbness lasted three days and nights.

Spontaneous remission is a change in perception—in this case a *sustained* change. This is a good example of a vision born of desperation. Desperation acts as the catalyst to make a dominant imprint. I have never had that back problem again! Was it a miracle or a coincidence?

I'm a skeptic, a doubting Thomas. I needed proof without a doubt, that Visionizing could make miracles happen. I don't like making a fool of myself. Dare I continue?

With the passion of a research scientist, searching for proof became my mission.

We have the power to choose and then we have the power to choose again.

"We fear that we are inadequate, but our deepest fear is that we are powerful beyond measure."

—Marianne Williamson (Often misattributed to Nelson Mandela.)

5

Turning Points

Before I ever knew what Visionizing was, I was already using it. Once I learned what Visionizing is, I reviewed significant turning points in my life. I recognized many of the various visions in my past experiences as proof that Visionizing works. I will point them out so you may do a similar review of situations in your life.

When I was about ten to fifteen years old, I hated my Outer World ego self. Girls called me "cute," "sweet," and "adorable." Guys called me "dummy," "queer," and "pipsqueak." Bullies beat up on me just for the fun of it. I was dyslexic, shy, fearful, and suicidal. I had no desire to be who I thought I was!

"Please, make me be *someone else*—anyone but me," I thought.

Imagine this little guy praying, "Please, make me be *someone else*—anyone but me." I was so adamant in my desire that I imagined myself being taken out of this body and put into another, as if changing bodies was as simple as changing clothes. Unknowingly, while praying, I was Visionizing.

One night the proof of what this Visionizing in prayer had imprinted surfaced for me when I had a vision born of revelation. Unlike in any ordinary dream, I saw a bright light looking more brilliant than the sun slowly approach. It stopped, and I heard a powerful voice say, "Do not pray for anything that is impossible for you to have."

Was it God answering my prayers? What happened to "faith can move mountains" and "ask and you shall receive"?

So where, you may ask, is the proof in this that Visionizing works?

Shortly thereafter, I had an, Inner World/Outer World change—an IWP-OWO experience. It was my first year at Eastwood High School. On the first day, as I walked up the hill to the front door of the school, a bully noticed that my blue suede shoes and pegged trousers were different from the white bucks and khaki trousers he wore. He called out, "Hey, your bus is going that way!" just as a bus went past the school. His buddies broke out with laughter. Needless to say, I felt unwelcome.

The entire student body assembled in the auditorium. On stage was a joyful, hot-looking guy who had been elected president of the student council the year before. He welcomed all the students back for the new semester. He kind of resembled me. Or was that just me, projecting myself?

In a power-moment of joyful identification, a vision born of inspiration, imprinted in me.

During the next year, I researched a dozen books on personality and on being popular. One revelation from my studies repeated in my mind until it imprinted: "Remember that other people have feelings, too! Remember that other people have feelings, too! Remember that other people have feelings, too!"

It was soon a matter of auto-control for me to treat the other students with the oneness of being another feeling me. In my senior year, there I was at the podium, smiling and welcoming all the students back for the new semester.

Eighteen and in New York City

Suddenly, I was an eighteen-year-old aspiring actor in New York City. I moved thirteen times the first year and spent several nights sleeping on a park bench while going to drama school, where I had won a scholarship. I finally found a job as a busboy in a Greenwich Village restaurant.

An older friend suggested I see an astrologer by the name of Bessie Lispenard. I remember one thing she said: "In your last life you were a priest." That was curious, because I had a strong desire to become a priest, but with the help of my objective intuitive inner voice, I had chosen to be an actor instead.

When I later went to Hollywood, an acquaintance invited me to the estate of a world-renowned mentalist by the name of Joseph Dunninger. Dunninger told me, "As an actor, I see a wall. You're going to be a writer."

Remembering how I cheated my way through all those high school spelling, vocabulary, and reading tests, I was amused at how wrong this famous Dunninger could be. I laughed and responded, "Uh, I bin in Hollywood for six months now, an' I din't even write my mudder a letter."

"Don't laugh. Not only are you going to be a writer, you're going to be renowned as one."

"Not likely."

As I was shaking Dunninger's hand and preparing to leave, he said, "In your last life, you were a priest in the hierarchy of the Catholic Church. When you passed on, things weren't as you had expected, and that's why you had to come back. You've turned away from organized religion in this life. Don't try to go back. It's not meant for you to do so."

Was this a coincidence or a confirmation of what Bessie Lispenard said?

Once the amazement passed, I dismissed it all. After all, I didn't believe in reincarnation.

But what if my birth really was my naked spirit-self putting on this Peter Copani body for clothing? Then death would just mean shedding this body, leaving my Objective Observer naked spirit-self, my decision-making intuitive internal voice, my fragment of a universal hologram—or any name we prefer to call it—to continue on.

That inkling of possibility certainly changed the landscape surrounding my life and what I called "death."

Journey into the Subconscious

In 1973, while still struggling with the fear that God was "punishing me with testicular cancer," I was wallowing in guilt. I was paranoid and claustrophobic, terrified of elevators, tunnels, flying—living—dying—and hell!

My analyst, Lee Mattiuzzo, guided me on a journey into my subconscious.

In my mind, I asked, "If 'the light' in my bedroom is in fact you, God, please—be with me now. I'm so confused. I don't want to be here. Save me, please." Suddenly, out of nowhere, I asked, "Doth not the father love the son as much as the son loves the father?"

The light appeared in my mind's eye just as it had in my bedroom eighteen years earlier: Once again I heard that familiar powerful voice: "Words need not be spoken and the fire doth not burn!"

What is the meaning or purpose in that? IWP-OWO.

Just when I was feeling blessed with a response to my prayers from the Almighty, my son, John-Vince, liked to say, "I think it's God's way of telling you to shut up."

A Jewish friend, Marty, told me, "The fire doth not burn! See? That means there's no hell! We're all children of God." It took me much longer to understand the "words need not be spoken" part. IWP-OWO. It is because the Creative Energy Force doesn't communicate through words but through images and emotions—an important part of the visionizing process. Our 'asking' as in "ask and you shall receive" is communicated through our Visionizing.

Being a child of God suddenly made a whole lot of sense. "Doth not the father love the son as much as the son loves the father?" and Marty's words became the material for a vision born of revelation—and it imprinted.

The outdated fear thoughts that were manifesting themselves in a suicide diet of fast foods, caffeine, sugar drinks, drugs, cigarettes, and other disease-causing agents were replaced with clear thoughts. These inspired a study of nutrition, fasting, healing herbs, and homeopathic remedies that spanned many works, including all of Dr. Gabriel Cousens's books; *Enzyme Nutrition* by Dr. Edward Howell; and *The Wheatgrass Book* by Ann Wigmore.

Soon I was manifesting a healthier "I want to live" diet that included fresh fruit and green veggie juices.

Battle against Arthritis Pain

Although I had been Visionizing in prayer for a year after I ran out of St. Vincent's Hospital in Manhattan, my fear of having testicular cancer drove me to see a specialist, an urologist named Dr. Hitzig. His tests determined that I had *no* cancer. Did the other three doctors make a mistake, or had a miracle taken place? Or maybe both!

Dr. Hitzig's X rays revealed that at the back of my neck, I had arthritis. This was in 1973.

"It's going to cause you a lot of problems as you get older," he told me.

I took the news with disbelief. "When they took the X ray, I had to hold my chin up too high, and that's why…"

"It's there, Peter. It's a very unfortunate and painful location to have arthritis."

In 1985, I refused medication for the arthritis that was causing neck pain. When I rolled my neck I heard a crackling, popping sound, but I was determined not to be on invasive painkillers or have my neck stiffen so I wouldn't be able to turn my head. I refused to accept the arthritis, instead focusing on visions of mobility while exercising and massaging the area. Finally, the pain diminished and disappeared. I forgot about having arthritis altogether.

A doctor reconfirmed the presence of arthritis from a lung X ray taken in 2005. I was amazed that the arthritis was there! The doctor was amazed when I told him I had no pain. Had Visionizing stimulated my brain into producing natural, pain-soothing endorphins?

Seek and you shall find. Ask and you shall receive—be inquisitive!

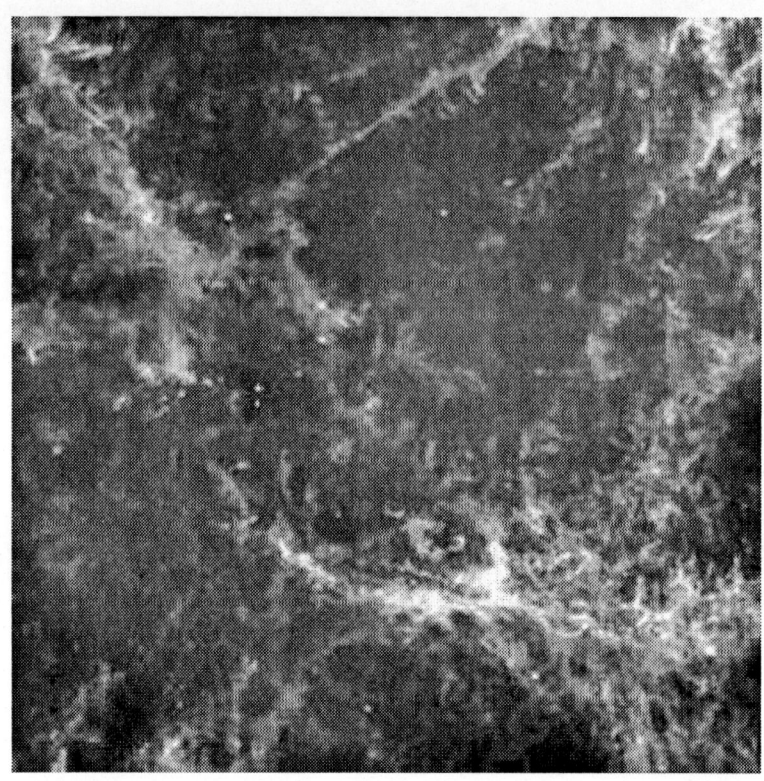

"Believe that life is worth living and your belief will help create the fact."

—*William James*

6

The Intuitive Internal Voice

The intuitive internal voice is a communication from our Objective Observer, our fragment of the universal Creative Energy Force, conducted through the universal mind thought system of oneness into our consciousness. It directs us for the purpose of clarity, identifying, knowing, and understanding. It is important for us to learn to distinguish this communication from the ramblings and contradictions of the ego mind thought system where confusion and separateness reins.

A memorable incident involving this internal voice occurred during my childhood. I was a war baby, filled with fears of air raids, bombs, borders, religions, and races. On the sofa, I would build playing card dwellings and imagine villages, towns, and cities, with card suits distinguishing races and their nations. In my mind, I proceeded to project playing card world wars. My hands became airplanes dropping card bombs. It became a repetitive game until one day when I heard that objective internal voice: "Why does there always have to be war, Peter? Why not peace?" I didn't understand the difference between the ego mind and universal mind at the time, but I learned to recognize that intuitive internal voice. Henceforth, inspired by that voice, my games became joyful visions of romance and unity concluding in celebrations of peace.

In the late 1960s, to learn more about myself, make a few bucks, and be helpful to others, I put an ad in a New York magazine offering intuitive psychic consultations. This is when I learned to trust that same intuitive internal voice that told me to run out of that hospital.

Before beginning a session, I would take a moment to "clear." That involved getting out of the ego mind and tapping into the "oneness" of the universal mind. I had to see my client as a universal being—complete, healed, and whole—and be in the universal mind thought system, where healing and miracles are commonplace. Recognizing that we are one universal being enables us to tap into the collective consciousness. When tapped into the collective consciousness it reveals itself as a source of material that becomes available in an intuitive or psychic experience.

While my client was present, I would pray, "If there's anything I can say or do that would be of help to this person, please, use me as an instrument of thy will." Putting aside the ego mind thought system made the way clear to access the collective conscious pool. Then I would feel confident to do or say whatever came to my receptive or cleared mind, whether it made rational sense or not.

An example of the results of this procedure is demonstrated in a session with Bob, a young father in his mid-twenties who came to me for a consultation. Bob sat across my desk just as I had done with Dunninger and began to speak. "I'm an exhibitionist," Bob said. "I've been in therapy two to three years now. It's not helping. I'm afraid of being caught and embarrassing my family, or worse."

"Sit on the couch there, Bob," I told him. "Tell me whatever comes into your mind." Only moments after he sat, he fell into a regressive state. His speech became incoherent. I waited.

Suddenly, I stood up, walked across the room, and in a confident and powerful voice said, "Who's Barbara and what does she have to do with this?" I spoke with confidence, just as though I knew what I was talking about.

I observed and waited as Bob lifted his head slowly. "Barbara is my mother's name." Bob revealed that he had regressed to a time when he was a child, naked and crying.

A Vision Born of Neglect

In Bob's vision, Barbara pointed to his penis and said, "There. See? You're a man." She was shaking him. "Now stop whining and crying and show Mommy you can be a man." She struck him, and he forced himself to stop crying. This vision born of neglect imprinted in Bob's Creative Force. Now, anytime Bob felt like crying it triggered an automatic response—djzz, djzz!—and he would refrain from his emotion, instead exposing that which proved him a man.

Here's another example of how many of us live our lives based on forgotten, outdated, and untrue imprinted beliefs.

One day a therapist invited me to sit in on a rehabilitation group session of people on parole for various infractions. I sat down and cleared with, "If there's anything I can say or do that would be of help, please, use me as an instrument of thy will." I listened while members of the group interacted. George had just finished saying something when suddenly I blurted out, "You're not a nigger, George!" The group was horrified. But George replied, "I've been called a nigger all my life, by both whites and blacks." The therapist looked at me and asked, "But how do we change it?"

I was able to hit the nail on the head and help both Bob and George identify the sources of their problems. Yet at this point, I could only identify obstacles; I didn't know how to help them resolve their conflicts. If I desired to be truly helpful, and I did, then I needed to research further.

How to overpower these past imprinted beliefs in three easy, mind-healing steps will be discussed in Chapter VII.

"I shall follow the path to wherever…my mission for truth shall take me."

—Kahlil Gibran

7

The Therapeutic Growth Process

I had finally recognized that *everything* in the Outer World is part of a natural therapeutic growth process. IWP-OWO. Inner World: Project. Outer World: Observe. It is unfolding inside our mind—*projected.* The purpose of the Outer World for us, as Plato would say, is to "know thyself." Events in the Outer World are not just happenstance or accidents. No such thing.

How we relate to the happenings we observe, participate in, or experience is an important part of our personal growth process. It is therapeutic and even, on a broader scale, the evolution of the consciousness of humankind. Healing through consciousness means coming into awareness of what is and has always been. It is the growth process of awareness. *All knowledge and truth already exists.* Only our awareness of it is growing. The purpose of growth in our Inner World is also for us, "know thyself."

As a street writer in the 1970s, I felt that I needed to get involved in what was happening in the Outer World so I could discover what was going on in me. I took it upon myself to go into drug-ridden and racially riotous communities in New York City. I had a specific purpose. For example, I was reading about riots between Italian and Puerto Rican Americans taking place in Brooklyn's Park Slope community. I developed a musical presentation using professionals at a community center with about thirty youths of Italian and Puerto Rican backgrounds. Rehearsals for the musical were more like group therapy. From the interaction, I developed the plot, characters, and the lyrics to the songs. This resulted in the show called *Street Jesus,* which dealt with racial riots. When I went into Inwood, Manhattan, we dealt with drug problems in that area through a show called *The Blind Junkie.* My purpose was to learn about myself and to alleviate tension by helping others transform negative feelings into a positive, creative experience using street theatre—like with the playing cards, only now with real people.

Dunninger's Prediction

In the summer of '74, I had sixty-two songs in three socially significant epic-musicals, all performing free to the public on the streets, in the parks, and at Lincoln Center festivals. Between one and four productions of my shows were produced each year for a decade off-Broadway, off-off-Broadway, and in street theater. During this period I calmed the battle in my mind, became drug free, and gained self-esteem. I also gained national recognition and became renowned as "America's leading playwright of the streets"—a fulfillment of Dunninger's prediction.

In 1978, just as I was on the brink of making money in the commercial the-atre, I was blackballed. I became despondent and depressed—an ego mind gut reaction.

I repeatedly asked the inner teacher for guidance. IWP-OWO. "What is the lesson or purpose in this?"

Becoming Financially Independent

Finally, I found a job paying $200 a week. I also found *Think and Grow Rich* by Napoleon Hill in a trashcan. I studied the content and recognized that the natural creative process I used to write my songs and this Visionizing process were one and the same. Once again, I put it to the test.

I enthusiastically began, not just saying the words but Visionizing. "I receive $500 a week…$500…$500…$500 a week!" As time passed, my overwhelming enthusiasm appeared more and more ridiculous. There was no sign of financial improvement.

Why, I thought, is this problem-solving, secret-to-success, health, wealth, and prosperity thought process working for some people but not for me?

I moved beyond my personal experience and searched both ancient and modern truth-seekers. For centuries, psychological and theological researchers have been telling us what Maxwell Maltz put most simply in *Psycho-Cybernetics*: "We move in the direction of our most dominant thoughts."

You have a thought? Let's say you're younger and are invited to a social, party, date, or dance. Remember?

You're getting dressed or ready to go.

"Oh, I don't *look* so good," you think. You immediately start to move in the direction of not going.

"What am I going to do? Watch TV?" You turn on the TV set. Then you start to think of the enjoyable social aspects of your event—the food, drinks, fun, and laughter. You move to go.

You're all dressed and ready, and you open the door. It's raining.

What now?

We move in the direction of our most dominant thoughts.

Keep in mind that it is the images and emotions our thoughts invoke in us that determines the direction we move in. Our Visionized thoughts dominate. The *most* dominant imprinted thoughts materialize first, and then the next, the next, and the next.

When your Creative Force is cluttered with past imprinted opposing "beliefs," you become confused or indecisive, and it takes longer for your newer visions to manifest. This is why when you're younger, many times your visions manifest more quickly, because you're carrying less emotional baggage or past, outdated imprints. You can see this in many of the personal experiences I've already shared with you.

Remember, the Creative Force manifests either thoughts that create illness—like when I was a schoolboy calling in sick—or thoughts that heal, like with my back.

Freud is often credited with saying, "There's no such thing as an accident." However, this sentiment has been repeated by many truth-seekers over the centuries. There is no such thing as an accident because the cause of the "accident" was long ago imprinted in our Creative Force and forgotten. Therefore, we think of the incident as an accident or without a cause when all the time it is the result of some forgotten past imprinted belief.

Research scientists at the University of Michigan, Princeton, and several other research centers throughout the world studying the placebo effect confirm that our thoughts manifest and actually influence the material outcome of whatever is being researched or sought after. This discovery is revolutionary. It may very well be the proof that we are indeed co-creators with our Life Force!

Many truth-seekers believe that our decision-making Objective Observer self chooses not only the time of our ego mind's body birth, but how and when our naked spirit-self is to leave our body. In other words, what we call "death" is pre-determined by us.

I dwelled on the works of two of my most helpful truth-seekers—Denis Waitley's *The Psychology of Winning* and Earl Nightingale's *Lead the Field*. I listened to the courses saturating my mind with their meaning daily, weekly, monthly, yearly. They added up to thousands of repeated attempts at imprinting the wisdom revealed in them.

Visions born of perseverance are the deliberate visions you develop. When you believe you've imprinted your vision, but you are not automatically going after it, that usually means that an opposing imprint exists in your Creative Force.

To sum up, I didn't realize that, like my client Bob, I had past imprinted beliefs opposing my vision of receiving $500 a week. That is, not until one afternoon when I was walking on the Avenue of the Americas in New York.

Bag Lady

Just ahead, I saw someone many people would refer to as a "bag lady." She was eating scraps of food salvaged from a public trashcan. I handed her a dollar bill. (*Djzz, djzz!*) She cowered like a vampire from a crucifix. "Aieehhh! Evil. Get it away! Aieehhh! Keep your money! Stay *away*!"

Extreme!

A woman walking past said smugly, "That'll teach you to mind your own business!"

I was embarrassed and humiliated by a crazy bag lady and a bitch—my angered ego mind reaction.

Then I thought, "What is the lesson or purpose in this? IWP-OWO. Is it just an illusion appearing real?" IWP-OWO. Testing. "What is it in *me*?" IWP-OWO. I repeated this action several times, searching my mind for the lesson or purpose in the incident. I was persistent in asking for the answer: "What is it *in me causing me to see this reflection out there. What is it in me?*" Inner World: Project; Outer World: Observe. IWP-OWO. Finally, I had "an awareness." That bag lady and I shared the same imprinted belief: "Money is the root of all evil."(*Djzz, djzz!*) Fear of being evil is the companion emotion.

That belief that was keeping that poor soul eating out of a trashcan was also keeping me piously poor and on welfare, preventing me from materializing my vision of receiving $500 a week to support myself and my fourteen-year-old son, John-Vince, who was living with me.

I researched and discovered an error in the translation of that well-known verse. The *love of money* is what the author (in First Timothy 6:10) intended to identify as the root of all evil.

Money Is the Root of All Good, When It's Used for Good

One step to undoing false or outdated beliefs is by Visionizing an opposing belief to overpower them. Consider: "Money is the root of all good…when it's used for good!"

I began to Visionize a wealthy and joyful me using my money to create a better life for myself and others. I would teach others to Visionize being healthier, more joyful, and triumphant by using this same Visionizing process. "Money is the root of all good…when it's used for good."

Thank you, oh thank you, dear bag lady for being my teacher.

After a year of Visionizing "I receive $500 a week," I was forced to resign from my $200-a-week job. The next week I began distributing free tickets to entertainment events needing extra audience. I charged a service fee for distribution, and by the end of that year I earned what averaged out to be $500 a week!

Is it just a coincidence?

More than just a job, that became the beginning of Audience Extras, an innovative service business twenty-seven years ago. Most of the money went to developing a communication system that would support the idea and the ever-increasing telephone bills, rent, salaries, computers, and other costs. Oh, how I dreaded paying taxes. That was a block.

I needed to change my attitude. I came up with another counter to my imprinted beliefs: "I love to pay my fair share of taxes. I want to pay a million dollars in taxes! That'll mean an increase in income!" I realized it was an honor and privilege to create jobs, stimulate the economy, and provide a service where everybody wins. *Everybody Wins* by Dorothy Jongeward is one of my favorite books.

Visionizing®

Visionizing the Resolution to Your Prosperity Challenge

Using the format of the third miracle-provoking exercise, you will create a vividly clear mental motion picture of yourself enjoying the resolution to any "prosperity challenge" on which you wish to focus.

(I'm including this miracle-provoking exercise in the form in which I guided people through it in my *How You Can Make Miracles Happen* live presentations, in the *Make Miracles Happen* CD, and in the Make Miracles Happen DVD.)

Every time I say "$10 million," you picture the resolution to your own personal prosperity challenge.

It could be any personal situation, relationship, or feeling that makes you better off. If you are looking for a lover or mate focus on the quality of person and how you feel in the relationship you desire. You actually create the outward image as a projection: IWP-OWO. Don't believe me? Where do you think "beauty is in the eye of the beholder" came from? If you are looking to mend a present relationship, the process is the same. Visionizing does not hypnotize others into doing your will. You need to Visionize the desired resolution in feeling while sharing time, adventures, and events in your mind's eye. It is very important to include the companion emotions for the imprinting. A gorgeous client asked me why every time she found a new boyfriend he turned out in the end to be "a nut job," as she described it. Her feeling of unworthiness was a magnet for abusive guys. These attractions are based on the imprinted companion emotion of how we believe we deserve to be treated. You can overpower any past imprinted belief beginning right now using this miracle-provoking exercise.

I used to believe that searching for the root of the problem was the way to go. Like in a "primal scream": go back to the original incident and cry it out. I remember meeting a friend who told me that she had discovered the source of her problems. "I've been crying for three weeks," she said, "I'm going to cry until I get it all out." It was believed by many that this was necessary for rooting out past problems. Knowing what I know about how the mind works, this truth-seeker believes that repetition further imprints the same old problem and reinforces its dominant status.

Remember the greatest secret of all time? What's the one secret that no one in power wants you to know. Over the centuries, people such as Nostradamus kept it to themselves for fear of being persecuted. Many people who possess it conceal it to use it only for their personal gain. Still others cloak or disguise it. They reveal it to you in bits and pieces, while charging you hundreds and thousands of dollars for the promise of revealing the entire secret to you. It is very powerful and, like nuclear energy, it can be used for both advancement and destruction. If it hasn't become clear to you so far, I will reveal it to you now. *We move in the direction of those thoughts we hold in our minds, our most dominant thoughts.* Our imprinted visions are our most dominant thoughts. It's not nuclear energy that makes the United States of America powerful; it is the freedom of thought or what some refer to as the *entrepreneurial spirit* that makes America powerful.

Having peace of mind, a dependable friend, a comfortable home, and world peace would be a priceless resolution of a prosperity challenge. Prosperity could also include having a peaceful, painless, and sudden transformation, for those of you desiring to leave the planet. Prosperity is literally anything that makes you *better off.*

Remember to include the companion emotion or sensation of your vision in the present power-moment of now.

If the resolution to your prosperity challenge happens to be money, then use whatever amount is enough for you.

Remember, I say, "$10 million." *You* Visionize the resolution to your own personal challenge. Always focus on the resolution—*not* the problem!

Recognizing our oneness with our creator and being in sound health is foremost. See, feel, and be your totally healthy universal self, like in the first miracle-provoking exercise.

Now, Visionize a triumphant and healthy you with your "$10 million," doing or having whatever prosperity means to you. Forget about any lack now. See, feel, and be the healthy prosperous you.

Think along with me, or maybe sing it: I have $10 million…a comfortable home…$10 million…a dependable friend…$10 million…whatever the resolution to your challenge…right now!"

You don't have to bore yourself to death doing this. It's okay to have fun. And why not? You're in the process of using a natural, God-given, miracle-provoking Visionizing process that works—if you do it right.

Visionize. See, feel, and be this very appreciative, triumphant, healthy, prosperous, $10 million motion picture of you in the present power-moment of now!

Directed by the components of your vision, the neurons in your brain are creating a thought pattern: "*Djzz-djzz*…$10 million…*djzz-djzz*…$10 million…"

Every time you repeat it, your new body cells are developing receptive ports to complement your new vision. Your hypothalamus is producing emotion-matching peptides that will stimulate your cells and alert your intuitive center to the opportunities for manifesting a triumphant, healthy, and prosperous you!

You could even tap dance to it, or tap your foot. "I feel healthy, oh so wealthy. I feel healthy and wealthy and wise…"

Where's your smile? You want the healing power of a smile, fun, and laughter. You don't want to manifest a sad, poor-me, unhappy "victim" face, do you? Forget about getting sympathy. It'll make you pathetic. "Oh, poor thing…"

Remember: "we move in the direction of our most dominant visions, so cling to the healthy, prosperous, and triumphant ones. Put joy in your visions and your life will become joyful."

Don't worry about where the $10 million is coming from. Just keep repeating your vision. Be persistent. You need to trust in the power within you. Very often your resolution will come from the most unlikely or unexpected sources.

Overcoming Obstacles

My good friend Donald Sharper had a limited formal education. He had been laid off from a twelve-year mailroom job and was looking for work. That was in 1980, just after I started Audience Extras. I told him I was working for myself and had started the business after a period of Visionizing. I explained the process more primitively than I am doing with you. He immediately was interested and started Visionizing. In just a few years, he founded the American Payroll Association, a very successful national service organization. He became a millionaire and fulfilled his dream, which was to travel around the world. And he did it twice!

If any past opposing imprinted feelings of unworthiness surface, like the fear of money being evil, they will block your new vision from sustaining manifestation!

Let's look at my client Bob as an example again. When in the universal mind thought system, Bob knew that real men sometimes cry. But when on auto-control, this reality became blocked or overpowered by his past ego mind imprinted belief that men don't cry. This was the source of confusion and inner conflict keeping him from progressing to his desired resolution.

Three Mind-Healing Steps

The following three easy, mind-healing steps have been created for clearing or cleansing ego mind blocks.

The first mind-healing step is to take an objective look at any problem, challenge, or situation you desire to resolve with the "Inner World: Project; Outer World: Observe (IWP-OWO)" formula. It is important to go through the motions described in Chapter III until the answer to your questioning surfaces just as I did in the example of the bag lady incident. IWP-OWO. Keep asking, every day and every night before going to sleep, until the cause of the block surfaces. Eventually, the cause does surface. Your Outer World illusion will weaken beginning with this recognition. Some truth-seekers call this process of dissolving or undoing the illusion, forgiveness. Forgive everyone involved, including yourself and move on. In the example, recognize the bag lady as a victim of a past imprint; recognize the woman passing by as an important part of the drama. Her being the "bitch" was to accent the importance of this situation for me in my life. So I forgive her for appearing to be the bitch! Then forgive yourself for being the victim of a useless outdated imprint. Take the responsibility which is yours or in this case, it became my responsibility to change it. If you are finding it difficult to forgive, remember that you are one with all creation and all others.

The second mind-healing step is to undo the illusory ego mind thought system by choosing to be in the oneness of the universal mind thought system, where healing and miracles are commonplace. How do you do this? By Visionizing in prayer. Prayer in itself is the calling upon the Creative Energy Force or nondenominational God. This is achieved by practicing the first miracle-provoking exercise. You need the clarity and perspective of the universal mind thought system of oneness.

The third mind-healing step is Visionizing® a new opposing vision to over-power any past, outdated imprints. The example is: "Money is the route of all good when it is used for good."

It all sounds simple, but it is most difficult to put into practice. How many of us have read a self-help or positive thinking book with every intention of putting it into practice, but instead we put the book down and just never do what we had intended. We are all guilty of this procrastination at one time or other. For this reason, I have urged you to perform the three miracle-provoking exercises while you read this book. Your personal desired resolutions envisioned during the exer-cises will linger in your Creative Force and coax you into repeating them. After many of the "How You Can Make Miracles Happen" presentations, participants say, "I feel better already!"

Oneness vs. Separateness

Visionizing is your tool to overpower *any* harmful guilt-causing, past, outdated imprinted attack thoughts. Many of these belong to age-old ideologies such as, "Women are inferior," "Gays are an abomination," and, "It's okay to kill the infi-del," meaning it's okay to kill those who do not think or believe as you do. These attacks are all based on the imprinted belief "I am separate from others and sepa-rate from all creation."

Separation is an ego mind illusion that teaches children to hate. For example, when a parent tells a child "Don't be like *they* are" or "Don't be like *those* people," this encourages inequality and catapults us into prejudice, ethnic cleansing, vio-lence, genocide, and war.

Every time a thought of unity or oneness surfaces, the dominant, existing belief that we are separate will sabotage it! As with the bag lady—djzz-djzz—our cells will default to the dominant, imprinted belief, in spite of our hunger for peace, unity, and sanity. It's like our bag lady teacher saying, "Oh no, stay away!" as she's eating out of a trashcan.

A lesson to remember is what many truth-seekers have been telling us. That is: We are spirit and not this body. Your body is a learning device for the purpose of communication, an ego mind creation; your body is the illusion in a dream.

The awakening from the dream is in the opposing vision to overpower the "I am separate" imprint. Choosing to be in the universal mind thought system means putting aside all things that divide. The awakening to reality is "I am one." It's an attribute of the universal mind thought system of oneness with each other and all creation, as demonstrated in our first miracle-provoking exercise.

Visionizing

Now please put aside all things that divide, like nationality, religion, race, sexual preferences, and monetary or class distinctions. I know this may be difficult at times, but please try.

Visionizing®

In your mind's eye, see, feel, and be yourself *worthy* of being a child of creation or of God—containing and reflecting the whole. Now see this reflection of you in others. Shorter, taller, poorer, richer, lighter, darker, believer, nonbeliever, older, younger, straight, bisexual, gay, male, female…Jewish, Christian, Muslim, Asian, Middle Eastern, Western, Indian! Without exception, leave no one out—*especially* not those you may have thought of as inferior or your enemy.

Look around you, past the façade, and think: "Another feeling me, another feeling me, another me, another, another, another feeling me."

Imagine your total universal self as one spirit, one human race; one world, in one universe; of one magnificent Creative Energy Force…one God almighty. (We're in an extension of the first miracle-provoking exercise here.)

Visionize® "I am one," until it is imprinted...djzz-djzz...until oneness becomes the *dominant* reflexive action. This forces the previous neuron network created by the outdated, untrue, imprinted illusions of separateness to retract like unused muscles, atrophy, and finally to decay.

See, feel, and be in the thought system of oneness. Think: "I am a universal being, free of all limits, labels, and judgments. I am complete and healed and whole. I am a universal being." Oneness is the wave of the future.

The hatred passed down through the ages can end here and now, through a complete and healed you. Peace begins with you united as one Universal Being—a mind/spirit/body self, sharing in the collective consciousness. And then it catapults outward. Inner peace: project; now observe...peace in your outer world. You are in the wave of the future: Inner World, Outer World, IWP-OWO.

Being selective of the thoughts imprinted in the Creative Force is one of the most difficult—and yet, most rewarding—dynamics to accept.

"Life becomes harder for us when we live for others, but it also becomes richer and happier."

—*Albert Schweitzer*

8

The Transformation

On my birthday in 1994, I received the first published copies of *Peter Copani's Handbook*. That same day, my son, John-Vince, was diagnosed with squamous cell carcinoma, a form of cancer. Doctors had found a malignant tumor at the base of his tongue and another under his nose.

After the shock, anger, and guilt of the ego mind passed, I asked, "What is the purpose or lesson in this illusion appearing real?" I practiced IWP-OWO again and again.

During this period my father and several friends left the planet. Mort, a good friend whom I had not known for very long, was one of those who shed his body. Only months later, his son joined him. I attended the son's funeral, a Jewish closed-casket affair. As I approached, I saw both Mort and his son above the casket dressed in vibrant white clothing, and Mort and I communicated telepathically.

Was the purpose of this vision a confirmation that we do not die?

John-Vince had three months of radiation and invasive neck surgery to remove infected lymph nodes. One lymph node had swollen to the size of a grapefruit. His neck didn't heal because of the radiation. Then they did another two operations—one to remove his breast tissue and another to use that tissue to make a patch on his neck in an attempt to keep an artery from rupturing. The trauma and drama were nonstop. We tried everything from the radiation to shark cartilage.

John-Vince refused to read my handbook until this point. It contains the beginnings of what I thought would be helpful to him. I hadn't developed a clear set of miracle-provoking exercises at that time. Even if I had, John-Vince wanted only to enjoy whatever time he presumed to have left. I was not consciously aware of how to Visionize in prayer on his behalf, although I did pray in the tradition I was taught as a child.

It became obvious what was imprinted in John-Vince's Creative Force when I heard him say, "No green drinks please! I know, I am what I eat, but I don't want to live the rest of my life a vegetable." And then he lit a cigarette!

"John-Vince, won't you please at least…try?" I pleaded.

"I want to party, go out and have some drinks," he said. "I know this is very painful for you, but please let me; it's my last hurrah." I respected his freedom of choice even though we both knew he was not to drink alcohol while taking all that medication. Much to his joy we went to his favorite bar.

A tumor was pushing John-Vince's eyeball out of the socket. The only thing the doctors could do would be to sew his eyelids together. They gave up on more radiation and suggested a hospice, but John-Vince, looking and sounding very much like the extraterrestrial in the movie E.T., said, "Home."

Somewhere in all that pain and suffering, the purpose emerged. My son and I recognized the oneness between us, illuminated in the form of unconditional love.

I had been selfishly praying he'd live. Now I prayed, "Please end the pain, take him quickly." I was powerless before John-Vince's imprinted vision. I knew not how to help him overpower it.

"With all the miracles I have borne witness to," I prayed, "is there no miracle now? Now that I need one for my only son? If there is anything I can say or do that would be of help to John-Vince, please use me as an instrument of thy will." I didn't have the advantage and clarity of the miracle-provoking exercises to bring the power of visionizing and the peace of mind invoked by practicing it.

The night before his transformation, John-Vince asked, "What was the name of that book I married all those people with?"

"John-Vince, it must have been the Bible."

He responded, as if remembering, "Oh, yes."

John-Vince's most mysterious question flashed through the neurons in my brain and presented me with what Bessie Lispenard and Dunninger had said. "In your last life you were a priest." It never occurred to me that John-Vince may have been a priest in his last life as well. I remember reading that we meet again in another life to resolve issues that were not resolved in a past life. I pondered whether John-Vince and I had known each other in a past life. We were always a source of learning for each other.

During the early hours of that morning my thoughts were shattered as John-Vince called out, "Oh the pain!" I was trembling as I injected the painkiller, Dilaudid. His breathing became irregular. I increased the dosage. The doctor gave me what was needed to end the pain and his life, as I knew it.

I held his hand as the pain subsided, and he released his final breath. I cried out with the tears I had been holding back for too long.

I sobbed at least three times every day for nearly two years. Doctors called it post traumatic stress disorder. If I believe that God created this world, then I must believe that this same God is the cause of all the pain and suffering in it. "Oh God, I hate you!"

The ego mind is a vain, cruel, vengeful, and insane substitute for a god. I was blinded with anger. Not knowing how to renounce this false god, I imprinted a death wish Visionizing a transformation within seven years. Inner World: Project; Outer World: Observe. I repeated IWP-OWO again and again. I began a suicide diet of junk food, nightly margaritas, caffeine, and Prozac.

On John-Vince's birthday, I spread his ashes. As I was leaving the area, I was stopped short in my tracks by the sound of his voice. "Thank you."

The purpose was clear. I was freed of all guilt and, once again, bore witness to the proof that what we call "death" is not "the end."

I told my doctor, who confided that he had had many difficulties with his mother; after her passing, he heard her voice say, "I'm sorry." I was relieved by this affirmation of my sanity.

I know John-Vince was plagued with guilt over an incident that took place when he was thirteen or fourteen. He broke into a grocery store, and at the sound of the alarm the owner had a heart attack and died. John-Vince's ego mind/false god judged him guilty of murder. Guilty of murder! The words "guilty of murder" repeated in his mind, even though it had been an unfortunate accident. This guilt became imprinted in John-Vince's Creative Force.

Remember, guilt demands punishment; punishment manifests fear; and fear of punishment manifests masochism, insanity, and suicide.

In retrospect, I recognize that it is this imprint of guilt that put John-Vince on auto-control for years of punishing himself to death. Suicide on the installment plan.

On several occasions, John-Vince talked about his guilt. "Do you think that God will forgive me?" he asked.

"John-Vince, I think you need to forgive yourself."

"How?" he asked.

Unfortunately, I just didn't know how to overpower past imprinted beliefs. And I didn't understand that true forgiveness is in the awakening from the ego mind's dream world of illusions.

Neither good nor evil, the ego mind is our creation. It is our teacher presenting us with lessons so we can awaken to who we really are. There is no god waiting to judge us. Earth is our projection, a "world book," from which to learn where we came from, why we're here, and where we're going.

Death is merely a transformation. So why are we so fearful of death? Because death is the unknown, dark and mysterious? We are not our clothes or the vehicles we travel in, and we are not these bodies.

What is the lesson in all of this? As long as I continue to live in this body, I know I must study this "world book." Does Visionizing really make miracles happen? Are there exercises or steps to follow? Then where are they? I can imagine myself turning the pages of the "world book."

My imprinted belief that "money is the root of all good when it's used for good" prompted me to start the Memorial Foundation for the Arts. The purpose of the foundation is to give grants to not-for-profit theatre companies in New York City in celebration of John-Vince's life and in recognition of the unconditional love between us.

Our Objective Observer naked spirit-self is created eternal. We don't die. We merely change clothes. What is the lesson or purpose in all of this pain and suffering? My perception changed. My anger was directed toward what I viewed as a cruel God, but over time the overwhelming feeling of loss turned to joy and a wholehearted thankfulness for the blessing of having John-Vince in my life.

Once I understood that we are responsible for our creations, the blame and anger I directed toward God diminished and finally disappeared. The healing is in the acceptance of responsibility for our creations. We are each other's creations. IWP-OWO.

"All the world's a stage, and all the men and women, merely players. They have their exits and their entrances, and one man in his time plays many parts..."

—*William Shakespeare*

9

The Ultimate Test

Finally, in the summer of 1995 another opportunity surfaced for me to prove that Visionizing makes miracles happen. I was diagnosed with hepatitis C. After several tests, including an MRI and a liver biopsy, it was determined that I had stage three advanced liver damage. It was estimated that my hep C infection most likely was contracted in the 1960s when I was experimenting with drugs and had progressed since. My symptoms included insomnia, skin lesions, itching, and fatigue. I showed signs of being in the chronic stages of the disease and was a candidate for the drugs interferon and ribavirin, both still in the experimental stages. Because one of the side effects was suicide, it seemed unlikely I would be taking it. I was already depressed and experiencing post-traumatic stress disorder (PTSD). The prognosis for what the doctor called "an incurable disease" included a progression to liver cancer, bone marrow cancer, liver transplant, and of course, death. It was recommended that I get on a waiting list for a liver transplant.

I needed another miracle!

With my life hanging in the balance, I put Visionizing to the ultimate test! The opportunity was very exciting, but also scary. I Visionized, "I'm healthy now!"

While browsing at Barnes & Noble, I picked up *A Course in Miracles*. A friend had shared the unpublished manuscript with me in the late 1970s. I bought the book and began an intensive study, this time using Ken Wapnick tapes and CDs on "the course" as a guide.

Over the next couple of years, my hepatitis C viral load increased. At this point, the doctor said I had advanced liver disease. Did I do it to myself? Yes! My death wish imprint!

Now the opportunity surfaced not only for the virus to attack my liver but also for me to prove once and for all that Visionizing works. That is, *if* it would work this time. How else could I prove the effectiveness of the miracle-provoking exercises and mind-healing steps without this hepatitis C virus? No *body* dies of good health.

I enthusiastically Visionized my desired resolution of being cured.

I heard my intuitive internal voice say, "Being helpful to yourself and being helpful to others is one and the same."

My alanine aminotransferase (ALT) blood tests of the basic function of my liver—or, as one doctor put it, "a measurement of liver cells dying"—showed results elevated 500 percent over the normal high reaching of 208. Disappointing news, but I joyfully Visionized a healthy functioning liver.

My viral load later increased to well over a million!

Very disappointing, but I passionately Visionized my desired resolution of being cured. I imaged Pac-Man eating the hep C virus. I also prepared a living will, requesting no life-sustaining equipment or measures. It's okay to use medication or magic to placate any doubt that Visionizing alone will work when it comes to the relief of any pain and suffering.

I chose the magic of interferon and ribavirin to control the disease in spite of my reluctance to use prescription drugs. I was plagued with side effects like fevers, insomnia, weight loss, paranoia, disorientation, and anemia, which caused more discomfort than the disease. I started injecting Procrit for the anemia caused by the interferon and ribavirin. I became fearful of overdosing on prescription sleeping pills, even though I had not slept for two months. I lost fifty pounds and looked like a prisoner in a concentration camp.

My "experiment" was getting out of control!

I began Visionizing, "I have a peaceful, painless, and sudden transformation." I couldn't remain focused long enough to repeat my visions most of the time, but I was persistent. While Visionizing, I felt and looked like a liberated and smiling concentration camp survivor. The death-wish imprint is powerful. Like John-Vince, I was on the verge of a long, drawn-out, painful, and not-so-sudden transformation.

In 2001, I discontinued all medication. What did I have to lose? I figured I was going to shed this body either way.

I chose to put the Hippocrates Health Institute (HHI) in West Palm Beach, Florida to the test. Hippocrates is an educational center where people go to learn how to live a healthier lifestyle, but many go there as a last resort when they have exhausted all allopathic medical treatments for their condition. The focus of HHI is on fasting, raw foods, wheatgrass juice, and the belief that we can heal ourselves with these remedies.

By the time I left Hippocrates in 2002, I was a certified health advisor, my ALT had dropped to twenty, and my liver was functioning in the low normal range. Impressive—yet what about the escalating army of three million-plus viruses, just waiting for the opportunity to attack my liver?

I prepared my last will and testament.

A Course in Miracles confirms what the ancient Egyptians, Hindus, Buddhists, Kabbalists, Sufis, and more recently scientists at the cutting edge have been saying all along. "The outer world is *our* illusion, not our creator's."

Then how do we forgive ourselves? By recognizing that our illusions have *in reality* never happened at all? How is that helpful? What does it all mean?

It means that just as I have the God-given power in me to create this illness-illusion, I also have the same God-given power in me to undo or overpower it. And so do you.

I repeated what was to become the first miracle-provoking exercise: "I am a universal being, free of all limits, labels, and judgments. I am complete and healed and whole, sharing in the collective consciousness of a magnificent Creative Energy Force embodied in the universe. IWP-OWO. I am free of all fear."

I chose to be in the universal mind by calling upon the nondenominational Creative Energy Force. "Please show me how, when I am united in you, there is no obstacle to my peace." I Visionized, "My immune system is healthy. I'm free of HCV. I am healthy, now!" I could see Pac-Man eating virus. I Visionized the resolution of myself being joyful and grateful to be free of the hepatitis C virus.

It had been seven long years since my diagnosis. Was it just "too late" for this opposing vision to be effective? I didn't want to opt for a long and painfully slow deteriorating existence. It was the quality of my life that was the issue here.

The key to recognizing what's imprinted in our Creative Force at any given time is revealed in our actions. Inner World: Project; Outer World: Observe. IWP-OWO. I can see, through my observation, that I put a supportive, new, healthy lifestyle into practice. A good indication that I was on auto-control to manifest my desired resolution was that I got plenty of beneficial before-midnight sleep. But my inner dialogue wasn't always so enthusiastic:

"Detox by fasting? I'd starve to death!"

"Exercise? Ugh, I hate it!"

"Too lazy to be healthy?" I forced myself to the gym four to seven times a week.

"Eight to ten eight-ounce glasses of pure water and green, leafy juices every day?" I thought I'd drown! But I drank it.

"Sea vegetables? Aargh…it's seaweed!"

"Wheat grass juice enemas…while standing on my head? Oh boy!"

"And organic supplements with *living soil organisms*! *Mmm, mmm good*!"

In October of 2003, all of the above and Visionizing myself free of hepatitis C materialized with an ALT count of twelve and a zero viral load. I have remained free of the hepatitis C virus to this day.

I still maintain a healthy lifestyle, except I've dropped the wheatgrass juice enemas. But if I felt the need to flush my inner organs with the healing power of wheatgrass juice, I wouldn't hesitate to stand on my head and do it.

Being selective of the thoughts imprinted in the Creative Force is one of the most difficult, and yet most rewarding dynamics to accept. Taking responsibility for our thoughts and actions is the secret for healing and the key to the resolution of all problems.

My experiences tell me "Visionizing makes miracles happen." Don't just take my word for it. Harness this natural Visionizing process and put it to the test.

It's one thing to *know* how to do the Visionizing process—it's another more difficult task for most people to actually *do* it. Remember, the power-moment is now! Enjoy co-creating your life. Have fun! Be healthy, be prosperous, and always remember you can make miracles happen.

Visionizing® Makes Miracles Happen

I am a universal being, free of all limits, labels, and judgments. I am complete and healed and whole, sharing in the collective consciousness of a magnificent Creative Energy Force embodied in the universe.

—Peter Copani

Epilogue

I have shared the miracles in my life with you and, most important, I've revealed how and why I came to co-create the three miracle-provoking exercises. The first miracle-provoking exercise is gaining a collective perspective of your Objective Observer naked spirit-self in relation to the Creative Energy Force—our creator or nondenominational God. The second miracle-provoking exercise is how to change your perception using IWP-OWO and asking "What is the lesson or purpose in this?" The third miracle-provoking exercise is Visionizing to obtain whatever you see as prosperity. The three mind-healing steps guide you to use opposing visions to overpower any undesirable or past imprints.

If you have been diagnosed with or believe you have a disease, get a second opinion from a medical doctor and an alternative health professional. Learn all you can about your condition.

Many people who come to the "Make Miracles Happen" seminars ask about hepatitis C. What helped me tremendously and what I did, besides listening to my doctor, was to find out everything I could about my liver: what it looks like, where it's located in my body, and so on. That way, when Visionizing I could create an accurate, healthy image of my liver. Always learn how the organs and body systems that are afflicted with your "dis-ease" function when they are healthy.

I searched through books to find which foods and herbs would be liver supportive. One would be dandelion. I learned that juices and raw vegetables were easier for the liver to digest—less work. I learned that fasting for one day a week would give my liver a well-deserved "day of rest." Then, I Visionized the connected afflicted areas and systems as healed, healthy, and functioning in harmony with each other, always Visionizing the desired resolution! I learned how important it is to detoxify or get rid of the disease-causing toxins in my system. This will tell you if you are indeed Visionizing a cure or giving up on this body and preparing for a transformation.

Many books and avenues to get information on fasting and detoxification are available, including nearly all the Bibles. Go to a naturopathic doctor or ask your healthcare professional if you prefer that route. You may wish to try using phytochemicals or natural healing properties contained in various herbs, plants, fruits, vegetables, and spices. The super-foods helpful in supportive healing of the liver include rainforest Acai berries, sprouted beans, sprouted seeds, sea vegetables such as chlorella, spirulina, kelp, blue green algae, garlic, and green, leafy veggie juices and wheat grass juice. I recommend doing your own research as well as checking with a traditional or natural healing nutritionist.

Busy your mind with getting the results you desire, even if it takes a miracle. Repeatedly ask, "How do I heal this disease?" IWP-OWO. Drink plenty of water to stay hydrated and to flush your system free of toxins each day. Explore any and all related holistic and alternative healing sources, such as shark cartilage. Even if you are to reject them, I suggest you know what your choices are. Some truth-seekers recommend starting each day with the juice of one organic lemon, eight ounces of water, and a couple shakes of ground cayenne pepper. You need to maintain a 7.5 pH alkaline-acid balance. Why? How does this affect your health challenge? Get all the facts, and then make a decision. Get all the information about the resolutions available for curing your "dis-ease," and when the doctor tells you it's incurable, don't give up. Be in touch with the intuitive internal voice by doing the first miracle-provoking exercise often. Ask for guidance using the second miracle-provoking exercise, IWP-OWO, while Visionizing your desired resolution (which of course means using the third miracle-provoking exercise).

You may choose any combination of the above. You may choose to take only the doctor-recommended medication. None will interfere with Visionizing the desired resolution to your predicament—especially when you need a miracle! Visionizing is the primary supportive healing process suitable for all occasions and is compatible with any bit of magic you may come up with.

Remember, you can tell what is imprinted in your Creative Force by monitoring your thoughts, listening to what you say to others, and observing your actions. IWP-OWO. Discover the lesson or purpose in your ordeal. IWP-OWO. Any change in perception can produce a miracle of a resolution.

After one of my "How You Can Make Miracles Happen" live presentations, I was asked what I would say to my client Bob to help him resolve his exhibitionist problem now? I would have Bob search his mind for a time when his mother, Barbara, was kind and supportive when she did allow him to cry or feel his emotions. Then I would help him take that incident and incorporate it into his Visionizing. If such an incident didn't materialize in a relatively short time, I would help Bob construct an opposing vision, which would go something like this: "It's healthy, appropriate, and manly to cry and express my feelings." And then I would have him proceed with the three mind-healing steps of Visionizing this opposing vision until it imprints as presented here in *Make Miracles Happen*.

There is just one more thing I would like to share with you, and that is the most valuable gift any person has given me. The bearer of that gift was Captain Robert Cook of the United States Army. He was stationed in Pearl Harbor at the time of the infamous attack. Captain Cook took the time to truly educate me—that is, to encourage me to *think* for myself. For that I am most grateful. He was the first person to present me with the idea that all of this Outer World may be an illusion created by each of us individually and all of us collectively.

He taught me to question with an open mind any and every idea, fad, law, decision, or dogma to be sure that it made good, clear, inner sense before I accepted or embraced it. "Is it right for me?" Put it to the test. View the world from every perspective. Take everything you have ever been taught and put it aside for a moment and ask, "What do *I* think?" What do *you* think?

My greatest hope is that I have shared a valuable gift with you in *Make Miracles Happen*.

When my nephew, Michael, was in the final stages of AIDS, I spoke with him of preparing for his transformation.

"How is this being positive?" he asked.

"It's neither positive or negative. You're identifying with your ego mind body. Your anxieties stem from a matter of mistaken identity."

"I thought they'd have a cure and save me from living with a terminal disease…and I'll miss Grandma."

Remember when I told you about seeing my friend Mort and his son over the casket? He was there for his son's awakening. I believe the purpose for that incident was so I could deal with John-Vince's transformation.

"We will be reunited again, Michael," I said. He smiled. "You are a child of God on your journey home. It's a time for setting your spirit free. You're not this body. It's your figure in the dream! It's okay to leave it behind. You're awakening from the dream. That is what the story of 'The Resurrection' is all about—to prove that you, and all of us are the one Son of God created eternal. We don't die!"

That was the last time I saw Michael before his transformation.

After repeating the first miracle-provoking exercise until it imprinted, and after Visionizing "I am One," my change in perception became the cure for my post-traumatic stress disorder. Imprinting "I am one" also became the change in perception resulting in gaining peace of mind and in alleviating the fear of what we call death.

Once you are aware of how the mind assimilates material, as you may have realized from reading these chapters, you can consciously take control of your thoughts in the present power-moment of now. If you remain a person who is unwilling to take responsibility for which information is imprinted in your Creative Force, there are many who are willing to take control and use it to get you on auto-control to do their bidding.

You now have the secret to successful living and a graceful transformation. If you still have any doubts as to how to make miracles happen in your own life, re-read this *Make Miracles Happen* book or, if you prefer, listen to the audio book or the *Three Miracle-Provoking Exercises* CD repeatedly until you are sure. For questions, supportive products, and further information about live Make Miracles Happen presentations visit www.mindhealingmiracles.com.

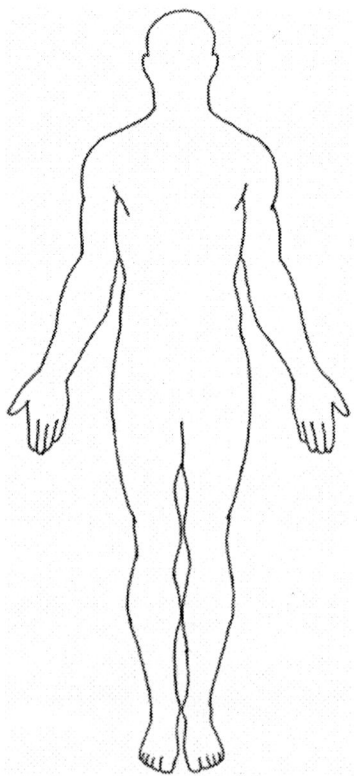

"My resurrection comes again each time I lead a brother safely to the place at which the journey ends and is forgot. I am renewed each time a brother learns there is a way from misery and pain. I am reborn each time a brother's mind turns to the light in

him and looks for me. I have forgotten no one. Help me now to lead you back to where the journey was begun, to make another choice with me."

—*Jesus in* A Course in Miracles *by Helen Schucman*

About the Author

Peter Copani is a certified Hippocrates Health Educator, an inspirational and motivational speaker, a health consultant, a metaphysician, and a teacher of miracles, Visionizing, and conscious co-creation, with over forty years of client experience. He is credited with making the way clear for many of his clients and friends to experience sound health, financial independence, and peace of mind.

Mr. Copani also has an extensive career in the entertainment industry. He has been credited with being "America's Leading Playwright of the Streets" in the *New York Times*. He is also the founder of three theater–arts organizations, People Performing, Audience Extras, and The Memorial Foundation for the Arts.

For more information, please visit www.makemiracleshappen.org, or contact Peter at:

Peter@mindhealingmiracles.com or at www.PeterCopani.com

APPENDIX

Song Lyrics

Throughout the 1970s people got to know Peter through the lyrics of his songs.

"God Is in the People"
(Copani)

I was hungry and you gave me nothing to eat
I was thirsty and you gave me nothing to drink
I was naked and you gave me no clothes to wear
I was sick and in prison
Suffering all alone
You didn't come to visit me
No, you weren't there
You didn't show me that you care…
And the people said,
When were you hungry
And we gave you nothing to eat?
When were you thirsty
And we gave you nothing to drink?
When were you sick and in prison
Suffering all alone?
How could we show that we care
When we didn't know you were there…?
And Jesus said,
In as much as you didn't do it
For one of these people among you
You didn't do it for me

Because
God is in the people
And the people are in God
God is in the people
To you this may sound odd
But God is in the people
And the people are in God
And the people said,
God is in the people?
And the people are in God?
God is in the people
It sure does sound odd
But God is in the people
And the people are in God...

"I Love the Sun"
(Copani)

I love the sun
It's my favorite star
I love the sun
Above everyone
I know this may sound odd
But the sun belongs to God
Who touches everyone
That's why I love the sun
I love the sun
It's my favorite star
I love the sun
Above everyone
Through Mother Earth
Blessed by Father Rain
The Sun of God
Helps the flowers grow again
I love the sun
It's my favorite star
I love the sun
Above everyone
All the flowers of the world
Each special in their own way
Very much like you and me
The sun loves them equally
I love the sun
It's my favorite star
I love the sun above every one.

"When We Are Together"
(Copani)

When we are together
We are the morning glory
Opening its bud
With a kiss from the sun
When we are together
We are the day, the night
There is no wrong
We're just right
We are the lightning in the midst of the storm
We are the cool and the calm and the warm
We are the rain kissing earth giving birth
We are eternity and all its' worth
We are all mystery
Solving riddle and rhyme
We are the sand
Marking time
We are a child
Awakened from eternity
We are the world
You and me

"Street Jesus"
(Copani)

Street Jesus
So hard to recognize you
Street Jesus
What are you trying to do?
Where are you now?
Are you wearing a disguise?
Will I know you when I see you?
Will I ever be that wise?
Street Jesus…Are you going to judge me?
Street Jesus…Do you have no pity?
Are you dressed as a woman?
Or do you look like a man?
Is the color of your skin
White, yellow, black or tan?
Street Jesus
Is that you playing bocce ball?
Street Jesus
Are you hanging-out in the hall?
Are you sleeping in a mansion?
Or on the bowery
Are you with a woman?
Show your face to me
Street Jesus
Is that you shooting up?
Street Jesus
Shaking a blind man's cup
Why do you wear a disguise?
Are you afraid of us?
I wanna be your friend
Not another Judas
Street Jesus

Are you singing a song?
Street Jesus
Is your hair short or long?

Are you playing dominos
And drinking Reingold beer?
Is it just a rumor
That you're really queer?
Street Jesus
Are you someone we should fear?
Street Jesus
Are you all of these people here?

"All Here"
(Copani)

Philosophy, psychology
E.S.P. and astrology
All here to help us see
That to know your own true feelings
Is to really be free
Science, chemistry
Biology and astronomy
All here to help us see
That the universe is technically
Very much like you and me
Loneliness, anger
Suffering and pain
Thunder, lightning
Tornado hurricane
Peace and hope
Love, contentment, and joy
Sunshine, rainbow
Starry night, summer rain
All here to help us see
The universe is technically
Very much like you and me
And to know your own true feelings
Is to really be free
A long-haired freak
A short-haired straight
Wearing clothing to suit their taste
To judge one another is just a waste
An issue that's gotta be faced
Now it's time to reiterate
Not to criticize but create
We can determine our fate

To know your own true feelings
Before it's too late
Loneliness, anger
Suffering and pain
Thunder, lightning
Tornado, hurricane
Peace and hope
Love, contentment, and joy
Sunshine, rainbow
Starry night, summer rain
All here to help us see
The universe is technically
Very much like you and me
And to know your own true feelings
Is to really be free.

"One of Us"
(Copani)

All the things, which divide
When you put them aside
Will it show…He's one of us?
Ethnically
A racial reference
Nationality
Or sexual preference
The shade of his skin
Or maybe his religion
All the things, which divide
When you put them aside
Will it show she's one of us?
We struggle to grow
Suffering for our sanity
Trying to fulfill our life
Our love and sensuality
Is he one of us you ask
Is she one of us?
What's the difference?
He hurts, she cries
He laughs, she tries
Feels good, feels pain
Then one day they die
All the things, which divide
When you put them aside
We will find…we are one
And if we look at the world as one nation
And all people as one human race
And get in touch will all of our feelings

There would be no doubt…
We are one…we are one…we are one…

"Wait & See"
(Copani)

If things don't look as good as they might
Put your arms around your baby and hold on tight
Everything is going to be just right
Because a human hand can change destiny
A human heart can set you free
Before it's done, we will all be one
Just wait & see
You say you're afraid of losing control
There's one thing you can't lose
And that's your soul
To know all life is just a goal
A human hand can change destiny
A human heart can set you free
Before it's done
We will all be one
Just wait & see
Have faith and hope and love
Humanity
The sun will burn out a billion years from today
Don't worry no one's lived that long anyway
Everything is gonna be OK
A human hand can change destiny
A human heart can set you free
Before it's done
We will all be one
Just wait & see
Have faith and hope and love
Humanity...

"Why Are We Here?"
(Copani)

Why are we here?
No thought to be small
Why must we try
To conquer all?
Why are we here?
Where will we go?
Why must we live?
We're all here to know
If we can feel
Love without fear
We'll find that beauty
Will always be near
If we can see
We're part of it all
It was meant to be
The dark, the light
It only takes a spark to ignite
With our own hand
To make us what we are
Travel to the moon
Or some distant star
Yet left alone
Ours to decide
Faced with a choice
Lose or rejoice
So what ever I am
If you must call me a name
There's only me
No one else to blame
If we can see
We're part of each other

All sister and brother
Day and night
Black, beige, yellow, red, or white
What ever I am
If you must call me a name
There's only me
There's nothing to blame
So if we can see
We're part of it all
It was meant to be
The tree, the park
The dark, the light
It only takes a spark to unite

"If Jesus Walked Today"
(Copani)

What would you do and say
If Jesus walked the earth today?
What would you do and say?
Would you treat him any other way?
If you met him on a bus
Would you push and make a fuss?
Ask him for his autograph
Or start to write his epitaph?
Or would you try to beat him?
Do all you could to cheat him?
Or would you call him on the telephone
And ask if he feels alone?
What would you do and say
If Jesus walked the earth today?
What would you do and say?
Would you treat him any other way?
If he spoke of loving each other
Would you call him your brother?
And if he were to talk to you
Would you ask him to heal you?
Or would you go betray him?
Plan to do away with him?
Call him by another name?
Or would you start to feel shame?
Or would you throw a stone?
Or make a crown of thorns?
Would you think he's working for the devil
And look to see if he has horns?
Would you deny him?
Clench a fist and defy him?
Or would you thank him for his deep concern

Bow your head to listen and learn?
What would you do and say
If Jesus walked the earth today?
What would you do and say?
Would you treat him any other way?
Would you treat him any other way?

"Spirit Am I"
(Copani)

Spirit am I
Your holy child my God
I am as you created me
Free of all limits
Safe and healed and whole
I trust in you
Free of all fear
One mind with my creator
Free of all sin
One with all creation
One self...
Spirit am I
Your sinless, guiltless
Holy child my God
Peace and light and joy
Abide in me
Free to forgive
Free to heal my world
Thy will and my will
My will and thy will
Thy will and my will
My will and thy will
Be One...

Reviews, Quotes, and Recognition

Peter Copani's Handbook, for People in Search of Love, Money, Power, Happiness, Inspiration, Sound Health and/or Peace of Mind is his bestseller. He has also written volumes on the teachings of Socrates, Plato, Aristotle, and Pythagoras, has translated into form scores of plays and epic musicals, and has had between one and four off-and off-off-Broadway productions of his work produced each year for over a decade.

Peter has received international recognition and won several awards for his work as a playwright and social activist. His epic street musicals became known as American street theater classics, and he is credited with seven productions of his work performed at the Lincoln Center Out-of-Doors summer festivals in New York City.

Many people came to know Peter from what the media had to say:

The *New York Daily News* called him, "The Bard of the Streets." Other media referred to Peter as "The Dean of New York Street Theater," "the Richard Rodgers of Street Theater," and "America's Leading Playwright of the Streets."

"Mr. Copani has been working successfully in street theater over the past few years as director, composer, writer, and den father, using as actors adolescents from some of the rougher neighborhoods in this city."

—The New Yorker

"In New York, Street Theater has come into its own as a viable urban summer stock. This is a unique theater form with unique sounds, unique surroundings, and unique audiences. The musical 'Street Jesus,' which played throughout New York this past summer, has proved Peter Copani to be the classic playwright for street theater.

—After Dark

The press on his Street Jesus production included the following excerpt from a *New York Times* editorial:

Street Action—*"In one area in Brooklyn, where racial rioting occurred last June 23, Puerto Rican and Italian teenagers have been brought together as a theater com-*

pany in an effort to alleviate the tension and instill understanding. The troupe, under the direction of Peter Copani and People Performing Co., travels the streets of South Brooklyn Park Slope spreading the theme of reconciliation."

"Mr. Copani's 'Street Jesus' was written for Puerto Rican and Italian Brooklyn teenagers to alleviate neighborhood tensions. And it did."

—Florence Fletcher, *The New Yorker*

"Mr. Copani's extraordinary gift for developing positive, artistic, and social events from potential community crisis by means of his distinctive approach to writing and directing young people, is certainly a talent and an achievement most worthy of recognition."

—Gordon Braithwaite, National Endowment for the Arts

At the formal opening ceremony of the Lincoln Center Out-of-Doors, Peter was presented with a city of New York Certificate of Appreciation by the Honorable Mayor Abraham D. Beame, which said: *"In recognition of his talent in working with the city's teenagers, his approach as playwright and director of young people developed a form that features community youths acting out real community problems. His creative success deserves the applause of all New Yorkers."*
Peter also received the following awards:

"For developing strong lines of communication through to use of the theater."

—Arts and Business Council Encore Award

"...For translating the dreams and fears of urban youth into beautiful and moving street plays."

—Washington Square Outdoor Art Exhibit Award

"Peter Copani has more productions of his plays done by street theater companies around town than Neil Simon usually has on Broadway. All his work bears a quality of vibrant ghetto life that in the view of many established critics, gives it a fierce blend of energy and substance."

—Steven R. Weisman, *New York Times*

"Peter Copani reveals an intuitive grasp of the heartbeat and idiom of the City's Streets."

—Mel Gussow, *New York Times*

"...Strong problem-solving ideas...In all ways wise, worthwhile, and winning!"

—ABC-TV

"Powerful"

—The Village Voice

But perhaps the sharpest possibility of street theater in the festival... "The Blind Junkie," a powerful, witty piece by Peter Copani, performed by a horde of kids of all ages, acting, singing, and dancing up a storm in their jeans, shirt-sleeves, tight dresses and sunglasses, and driven by a great soul-rock score...This show, with its bitterness, humor, and absolute wisdom about ghetto realities from cops to drugs to sex to welfare."

—Jack Kroll of Newsweek Magazine

In the 1970s, Peter developed and conducted a special self-esteem building program for welfare recipients in New York City.

He has served as a professional psychic/intuitive consultant to people from many walks of life for over two decades.

Mr. Copani has been awarded inclusion in The International Who's Who Of Intellectuals as well as *Men of Achievement* in recognition of his distinguished achievements. He is also included in the *Who's Who in America: The Notable Americans of The Bicentennial Era* edition.

Peter Copani has appeared on several television and radio shows in America, including Midday Live, and many radio news programs. He has been on the ABC, CBS, and NBC networks. He has been featured in news and magazine articles in the *Saturday Review, New York Times*, and *Newsweek* to mention a few. He has been the sole topic of several radio and television shows produced by and for European television, including a *Voice of America* radio program aired behind the Iron Curtain and a New York State Board of Education television documentary.

Selected References

Briggs, John C. and Peat, F. David. *The Looking Glass Universe*. New York: Simon & Schuster, June, 1986.

Copani, Peter. *Peter Copani's Handbook For People in Search of Love, Money, Power, Happiness, Inspiration, and/or Peace Of Mind*. Florida: Rainbow Books, 1993.

Cousens, Gabriel, M.D. *Conscious Eating*. California: North Atlantic Books, 2000.

Foundation for Inner Peace. *A Course In Miracles*. New York: Penguin Books, 1996.

Gibran, Kahlil. *The Prophet*. New York: Knopf, September 12, 1923, *The Secrets of The Heart*. New York: Carol Publishing Corporation, July, 1992, and *Voice of The Master*. New York: Citadel Press, June, 1963.

Hesse, Hermann. *Siddhartha*. New York: New Directions Publishing Corporation, 1951.

Hill, Napoleon. *Think and Grow Rich*. New York: Fawcett Crest, July, 1960.

Howell, Edward, M.D. *Enzyme Nutrition*. New Jersey: Avery Publishing Group, Inc., 1985.

Jongeward, Dorothy. *Everybody Wins*. New York: Addison-Wesley Publishing, 1973.

Karbo, Joe. *The Lazy Man's Way to Riches*. California: F P Publishing Co., January, 1973.

Kübler-Ross, Elisabeth. *On Death and Dying*. New York: Touchstone, 1997.

Lipton, Bruce H. *The Biology of Belief*. California: Mountain of Love/Elite Books, 2005.

Maltz, Maxwell, M.D. *Psycho-Cybernetics*. New York: Pocket Books, May, 1969.

Pert, Candace B. *Molecules of Emotion*. New York: Touchstone, 1999.

Rubin, Jordan S., N.M.D., C.N.C. *Patient Heal Thyself*. California: Freedom Press, 2003.

Siegel, Bernie S. *Love, Medicine, and Miracles: Lessons Learned about Self-healing from a Surgeon's Experience with Exceptional Patients*. New York: Harper & Row, 1986.

Stern, Jess. *Edgar Cayce: The Sleeping Prophet*. New York: Bantam Books, February, 1982.

Swedenborg, Emanuel. *Divine Love and Wisdom*. Swedenborg Foundation, March 1, 2003, and *The Divine Providence*. Swedenborg Foundation, June 2003.

Talbot, Michael. *The Holographic Universe*. New York: Harper Perennial, May 6, 1992.

Walsch, Neale Donald. *Conversations with God: An uncommon dialogue* (books 1, 2, and 3). New York: G.P. Putnam's Sons, 1996.

Wigmore, Ann. *The Wheatgrass Book*. New Jersey: Avery Publishing Group, Inc., 1985.

Zukav, Gary. *The Dancing Wu Li Masters*. New York: Bantam Books, August, 1980, and *Seat of the Soul*. New York: Fireside, 1990.

978-0-595-37970-5
0-595-37970-2

Printed in the United States
59440LVS00006B/1-204

9 780595 379705